LINE by LINE

STORIES FOR LEARNERS OF ENGLISH

SECOND EDITION

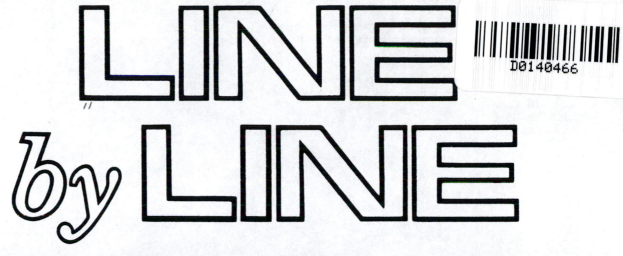

INTERMEDIATE

Steven J. Molinsky / Bill Bliss

PRENTICE HALL REGENTS
Englewood Cliffs, New Jersey 07632

Library of Congress Cataloging-in-Publication Data

Molinsky, Steven J.
   Line by line : stories for learners of English : intermediate /
Steven J. Molinsky, Bill Bliss. — 2nd ed.
      p.   cm.
   "Consists of the reading selections and accompanying exercises
contained in Side by side, second edition: books 3 and 4"—P.
   Includes index.
   ISBN 0-13-536889-8
   1. English language—Textbooks for foreign speakers.
2. Readers—1950-   I. Bliss, Bill.   II. Molinsky, Steven J.   Side
by side.   III. Title.
PE1128.M69   1991
428.6'4—dc20
                                        90-21683
                                        CIP

Editorial/production supervision: Kala Dwarakanath
Pre-Press buyer: Ray Keating
Manufacturing buyer: Lori Bulwin
Cover and interior design: Kenny Beck

Illustrated by Richard E. Hill

© 1991 by Prentice-Hall, Inc.
A Simon & Schuster Company
Englewood Cliffs, New Jersey 07632

Printed in the United States of America

10 9 8 7 6 5 4 3

ISBN 0-13-536889-8

Prentice-Hall International (UK) Limited, *London*
Prentice-Hall of Australia Pty. Limited, *Sydney*
Prentice-Hall Canada Inc., *Toronto*
Prentice-Hall Hispanoamericana, S.A., *Mexico*
Prentice-Hall of India Private Limited, *New Delhi*
Prentice-Hall of Japan, Inc., *Tokyo*
Simon & Schuster Asia Pte. Ltd., *Singapore*
Editora Prentice-Hall do Brasil, Ltda., *Rio de Janeiro*

To the Teacher

Line by Line: Intermediate consists of the reading selections and accompanying exercises contained in *Side by Side Second Edition: Books 3 and 4*. It is designed to serve as a supplementary or stand-alone reader.

The goal of *Line by Line* is to provide meaningful, relevant, and enjoyable reading practice while offering a clear, intensive focus on specific aspects of English grammar. The readings depict a wide range of characters and everyday life situations—many dealing with key adult lifeskill competencies, such as food, employment, health, housing, shopping, and transportation.

AN OVERVIEW

Chapter Opening Pages

The opening page of each chapter provides an overview of the grammatical structures treated in the chapter.

Reading Selections

Short reading selections offer enjoyable reading practice that simultaneously reinforces specific grammatical structures. Accompanying illustrations serve as visual cues that guide learners through the reading, helping to clarify both context and new vocabulary.

Check-Up

Check-Up exercises provide focused practice in reading comprehension and vocabulary development. Also, listening exercises enable students to develop their aural comprehension skills through a variety of listening activities.

How About You?

How About You? activities are intended to provide students with opportunities to apply lesson content to their own lives and experiences and to share opinions in class.

In Your Own Words

These activities provide topics and themes for student compositions and classroom discussions. Students write about their friends, families, homes, schools, jobs, and themselves.

SUGGESTED TEACHING STRATEGIES

Introducing Reading Selections

You may wish to preview each story either by briefly setting the scene or by having students talk about the illustrations or predict the content of the story from the title. You may also find it useful to introduce beforehand any vocabulary you think your students might be unfamiliar with. On the other hand, you may prefer to skip the previewing step, and instead have students experience the subject matter and any unfamiliar words in the context of the initial reading of the story.

There are many ways in which students can read and talk about the stories. Students may read silently to themselves or follow along as the story is read by you, by one or more students, or on the tape. You should then ask students if they have any questions and check understanding of vocabulary.

Q & A Exercises

Q & A exercises are included as part of the Check-Up after many of the reading selections. These exercises are designed to give students conversation practice based on information contained in the stories. Italic type is used in the Q & A model to highlight which words get replaced by different information contained in the reading.

Call on a pair of students to present the Q & A model. Have students work in pairs to create new dialogs based on the model, and then call on pairs to present their new dialogs to the class.

In Your Own Words

These activities are designed to guide students in their creation of original stories. Students are asked to write about topics such as their homes, schools, friends, families, and themselves.

You should go over the instructions for the activities and make sure students understand what is expected. Students should then write their stories, taking sufficient time to think about what they want to say, using a dictionary for any new words they wish to include. These activities are perhaps most appropriately assigned for homework to guarantee that all students will have sufficient time to develop their ideas and write them out.

Many teachers will find these written pieces a basis for effective peer work in class. Students can work together, telling their stories to each other, asking and answering questions about the stories, and correcting each other's written work.

As a final step, the *In Your Own Words* activities serve as a vehicle for classroom speaking practice. Students can tell their own stories, or perhaps tell the stories of their "peer-work" partners, while the rest of the class listens and asks questions.

In conclusion, we have attempted to help students develop their reading and writing abilities in English through a collection of carefully structured stories that are both lighthearted in content and relevant to students' lives. While we hope that we have conveyed to you the substance of our textbook, we also hope that we have conveyed the spirit: that the study of reading and writing can be dynamic...communicative...and fun!

Steven J. Molinsky
Bill Bliss

Contents

Review:
Simple Present Tense
Present Continuous Tense
Subject Pronouns
Object Pronouns
Possessive Adjectives

Practicing

PRACTICING

My sisters, my brother, and I are busy this afternoon. We're staying after school, and we're practicing different things.

I'm practicing tennis. I practice tennis every day after school. My tennis coach tells me I'm an excellent tennis player, and my friends tell me I play tennis better than anyone else in the school. I want to be a professional tennis player when I grow up. That's why I practice every day.

My brother Jimmy is practicing football. He practices football every day after school. His football coach tells him he's an excellent football player, and his friends tell him he plays football better than anyone else in the school. Jimmy wants to be a professional football player when he grows up. That's why he practices every day.

My sister Susan is practicing the violin. She practices the violin every day after school. Her music teacher tells her she's an excellent violinist, and her friends tell her she plays the violin better than anyone else in the school. Susan wants to be a professional violinist when she grows up. That's why she practices every day.

My sisters Patty and Melissa are practicing ballet. They practice ballet every day after school. Their dance teacher tells them they're excellent ballet dancers, and their friends tell them they dance ballet better than anyone else in the school. Patty and Melissa want to be professional ballet dancers when they grow up. That's why they practice every day.

✔ CHECK-UP

Q & A

You're talking with the person who told the story on page 2. Using this model, create dialogs based on the story.

A. What's *your brother Jimmy* doing?
B. *He's* practicing *football.*
A. *Does he* practice very often?
B. Yes, *he does.* *He practices* every day after school.
A. *Is he* a good *football player*?
B. Yes, *he is. His football coach* says *he's* excellent, and *his* friends tell *him he plays football* better than anyone else in the school.

Listening

Listen and choose the best answer.

1. a. I practice the piano.
   b. I'm practicing the piano.

2. a. Yes, I am.
   b. Yes, I do.

3. a. Yes, I am.
   b. Yes, I do.

4. a. He cooks dinner.
   b. He's cooking dinner.

5. a. My husband cooks.
   b. My husband is cooking.

6. a. No, they aren't.
   b. No, they don't.

7. a. Yes, when he grows up.
   b. Yes, when she grows up.

8. a. Yes, you are.
   b. Yes, we are.

9. a. Yes. She's a very good singer.
   b. Yes. She's a very good swimmer.

10. a. He's reading the newspaper.
    b. He's eating spaghetti.

✏ IN YOUR OWN WORDS

For Writing and Discussion

Tell about studying English.

Do you go to English class? Where?
When do you go to class?
What's your teacher's name?
Do you practice English after class?
  How do you practice?
  Who do you practice with?

2

Review:
Simple Past Tense
(Regular and Irregular Verbs)
Past Continuous Tense
Difficult Experiences

DIFFICULT EXPERIENCES

Miss Henderson usually teaches very well, but she didn't teach very well this morning. In fact, she taught very badly. While she was teaching, her supervisor was sitting at the back of the room and watching her. It was a very difficult experience for Miss Henderson. She realized she wasn't teaching very well, but she couldn't do anything about it. She was too nervous.

Stuart usually types very well, but he didn't type very well today. In fact, he typed very badly. While he was typing, his boss was standing behind him and looking over his shoulder. It was a difficult experience for Stuart. He realized he wasn't typing very well, but he couldn't do anything about it. He was too upset.

The Johnson Brothers usually sing very well, but they didn't sing very well last night. In fact, they sang very badly. While they were singing, their parents were sitting in the audience and waving at them. It was a difficult experience for the Johnson Brothers. They realized they weren't singing very well, but they couldn't do anything about it. They were too embarrassed.

The President usually speaks very well, but he didn't speak very well this afternoon. In fact, he spoke very badly. While he was speaking, several demonstrators were standing at the back of the room and shouting at him. It was a difficult experience for the President. He realized he wasn't speaking very well, but he couldn't do anything about it. He was too angry.

✔CHECK-UP

Q & A

Miss Henderson, Stuart, the Johnson Brothers, and the President are talking with friends about their difficult experiences. Using this model, create dialogs based on the story on page 6.

A. You know...*I* didn't *teach* very well *this morning.*
B. You didn't?
A. No. In fact, *I taught* very badly.
B. I *don't* understand. You usually *teach* VERY well. What happened?
A. While *I was teaching, my supervisor was sitting at the back of the room and watching me.*
B. Oh. I bet that was a very difficult experience for you.
A. It was. *I was* very *nervous.*

Match

We often use colorful expressions to describe how we feel. Try to match the following expressions with the feelings they describe.

_F_ 1. "My stomach is growling."	a. angry
_c_ 2. "I can't keep my eyes open."	b. embarrassed
_h_ 3. "I'm jumping for joy!"	c. bored
_e_ 4. "I'm seeing red!"	d. nervous
_b_ 5. "I'm ashamed to look at them straight in the eye."	e. scared
_A_ 6. "I'm on pins and needles!"	f. hungry
_d_ 7. "I'm shaking like a leaf!"	g. sad
_g_ 8. "I'm feeling blue."	h. happy

IN YOUR OWN WORDS

For Writing and Discussion

A DIFFICULT EXPERIENCE

Tell about a difficult experience you had.

What happened?
How did you feel?

✔ CHECK-UP

What's the Word?

I. Fill in the correct words and then practice the conversation.

A. _Were_ you sleep well last night?

B. No, I _wasn't_. I _was_ too excited.

A. Oh? Why _were_ you excited?

B. I _was_ thinking about the job interview I had yesterday afternoon.

A. Oh? _did_ you go to an interview yesterday?

B. Yes, I _did_.

A. _Were_ you nervous?

B. No, I _wasn't_. The interviewer _was_ very nice, and she ____ ask me any difficult questions.

A. ____ you get the job?

B. I ____ know yet. I'll find out today or tomorrow.

II. Choose the correct words to complete the questions and answers.

argue	bake	break	burn	cut	get
lose	meet	play	shop	slice	work

1. A. How did Ted _break_ his leg?
   B. He _broke_ it while _he_ _was_ _playing_ soccer.

2. A. How did Barbara ____ her purse?
   B. She ____ it while ____ ____ ____ at the supermarket after work today.

3. A. How did Jimmy ____ a bloody nose?
   B. He ____ it while ____ ____ ____ with the boy across the street.

4. A. How did Carol ____ the President?
   B. She ____ him while ____ ____ ____ in Washington.

5. A. How did Roger ____ his finger?
   B. He ____ it while ____ ____ ____ tomatoes.

6. A. How did you ____ yourself?
   B. I ____ myself while ____ ____ ____ cookies for my daughter and her friends.

Listening

Listen and choose the best answer.

1. a. Yes, I did.
   b. Yes, I was.

2. a. They cleaned their rooms.
   b. They were cleaning their rooms.

3. a. She played basketball.
   b. She was playing basketball.

4. a. He was nervous.
   b. He was looking over his shoulder.

5. a. I was bored.
   b. You were bored.

6. a. I was very hungry.
   b. I wasn't very hungry.

Review:
Future: Going to
Future: Will
Future Continuous Tense

Plans for the Weekend

Saying Good-bye

READING

PLANS FOR THE WEEKEND

It's Friday afternoon, and all the employees at the Acme Insurance Company are thinking about their plans for the weekend. Doris is going to plant flowers in her yard. Michael is going to paint his house. Tom and Jane are going to go to the beach. Peter is going to play baseball with his children. Rita is going to go camping in the mountains. And Karen and her friends are going to have a picnic.

Unfortunately, the employees at the Acme Insurance Company are going to be very disappointed. According to the radio, it's going to rain cats and dogs all weekend.

✔CHECK-UP

Q & A

The employees of the Acme Insurance Company are talking with each other. Using this model, create dialogs based on the story.

A. Tell me, *Doris,* what are you going to do this weekend?
B. I'm going to *plant flowers in my yard.* How about YOU, *Michael?* What are YOU going to do?
A. I'm going to *paint my house.*
B. Well, have a nice weekend.
A. You, too.

What are you going to do this weekend? What's the weather forecast?

Listening

Listen to the conversation and choose the answer that is true.

1. a. He's going to wear his blue suit.
   b. He's going to wear his black suit.

2. a. He's going to make spaghetti and meatballs for dinner.
   b. He's going to make beef stew for dinner.

3. a. They're going to go to the movies.
   b. They're going to watch TV.

4. a. He's going to go to the supermarket tomorrow.
   b. He's going to work in his garden tomorrow.

5. a. He's going to call a mechanic.
   b. He's going to call a plumber.

6. a. They're going to buy the car.
   b. They aren't going to buy the car.

SAYING GOOD-BYE

Mr. and Mrs. Anastas are at the Athens Airport. They're saying good-bye to their son Dimitri and his family. It's a very emotional day. In a few minutes, Dimitri and his family will get on a plane and fly to the United States. They won't be coming back. They're leaving Greece permanently, and Mr. and Mrs. Anastas won't be seeing them for a long, long time.

Dimitri and his family are going to live in Chicago. They're going to stay with his wife's relatives. Dimitri will work in the family's restaurant. His wife, Anna, will take any job she can find during the day, and she'll study English at night. The children will begin school in September.

Mr. and Mrs. Anastas are both happy and sad. They're happy because they know their son and his family will have a good life in their new home. However, they're sad because they know they're going to be very lonely. Their house will be quiet and empty, they'll have to celebrate holidays by themselves, and they won't see their grandchildren grow up.

Some day Mr. and Mrs. Anastas will visit Chicago, or perhaps they'll even move there. But until then, they're going to miss their family very much. As you can imagine, it's very difficult for them to say good-bye.

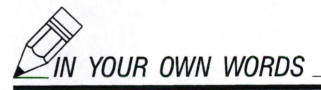

✔CHECK-UP

True or False?

1. Dimitri and his family will be leaving Greece for a few minutes.
2. Anna's relatives live in Chicago.
3. Mr. Anastas is happy and Mrs. Anastas is sad.
4. Mr. and Mrs. Anastas might move to Chicago.
5. Mr. and Mrs. Anastas are sad because they'll be at the Athens Airport until they visit Chicago or move there.

IN YOUR OWN WORDS

For Writing and Discussion

1. Tell about an emotional day in your life when you had to say good-bye.
2. Tell about your plans for the future.

   How long are you going to study English?
   What are you going to do after you finish?
   What kind of work are you going to do?
   Where are you going to live?

Present Perfect Tense

We Can't Decide

Working Overtime

Sharon Likes New York

READING

WE CAN'T DECIDE

My friends and I can't decide what to do tonight. I don't want to see a movie. I've already seen a movie this week. Jack doesn't want to go bowling. He has already gone bowling this week. Nancy doesn't want to eat at a restaurant. She has already eaten at a restaurant this week. Betsy and Philip don't want to play cards. They have already played cards this week. And NOBODY wants to go dancing. We have all gone dancing this week.

It's already 9 P.M., and we still haven't decided what we're going to do tonight.

✔ CHECK-UP

Group Conversation

You and other students in your class are the people in this story. In a small group, create a group conversation. Use the lines below to get your conversation started.

A. Look! It's already 9 P.M., and we still haven't decided what we're going to do tonight. Does anybody have any ideas?
B. I don't know.
C. Do you want to see a movie?
D. No, not me. I've already . . .
E. Does anybody want to . . . ?
F. I don't. I've already . . .
G. I have an idea. Let's . . .
H. No, I don't want to do that. I've already . . .

What's the Word?

Fill in the correct words to complete the story.

Alvin has a very bad cold. He has felt* miserable all week, and he still feels miserable now. He's very upset. He has tried very hard to get rid of his cold, but nothing he has done has helped. At the beginning of the week, he went to a clinic and saw a doctor. He followed the doctor's advice all week. He stayed home, took aspirin, drank† orange juice, ate chicken soup, and rested in bed.

At this point, Alvin is extremely frustrated. Even though he has _____ to a clinic and _____ a doctor, _____ home, _____ aspirin, _____ orange juice, _____ chicken soup, and _____ in bed, he STILL has a very bad cold. Nothing he has _____ has helped.

We hope you feel better soon, Alvin!

*feel–felt–felt
†drink–drank–drunk

14

WORKING OVERTIME

I'm an employee of the Goodwell Computer Company. This is a typical Friday afternoon at our office. All the employees are working overtime. We haven't gone home because we haven't finished our work yet. Friday is always a very busy day.

The secretary still hasn't typed two important letters. The bookkeeper hasn't written all the paychecks. The office clerks haven't delivered all the mail. And the boss still hasn't spoken to three important people who are waiting to see him.

As for me, I'm the custodian, and I haven't finished my work yet either. I still haven't cleaned all the offices because my co-workers haven't gone home yet! I'm not really surprised. Friday is always a very busy day at our office.

✔ CHECK-UP

Q & A

The custodian at the Goodwell Computer Company is talking with the employees on a typical Friday afternoon. Using this model, create dialogs based on the story.

A. I see you haven't gone home yet.
B. No, I haven't. I still haven't *typed two important letters.*
A. Well, have a good weekend.
B. You, too.

What's the Word?

1. A. Have you (see) _____ the letter from the Acme Company?
   B. Yes. I _____ it on your desk.

2. A. Have you (eat) _____ lunch yet?
   B. Yes. I _____ a few minutes ago.

3. A. Has the bookkeeper (go) _____ to the bank yet?
   B. Yes, she _____. She _____ there this morning.

4. A. Have you (speak) _____ to the boss about your vacation?
   B. Yes, I _____. I _____ to her about it yesterday.

5. A. Have you (make) _____ plans for my trip to Chicago yet?
   B. Yes. I _____ them yesterday.

6. A. Has anybody (read) _____ today's *New York Times*?
   B. Yes. I _____ it on my way to work.

7. A. Has the office clerk (take) _____ the mail to the post office yet?
   B. No, he _____. He _____ it to the mail room ten minutes ago, but _____ _____ _____ it to the post office yet.

8. A. Has John (finish) _____ his work for the day?
   B. Yes, he _____. He's already (go) _____ home.

READING

SHARON LIKES NEW YORK

Sharon has lived in New York for a long time. She has done a lot of things in New York. She has seen several plays, she has gone to the top of the Empire State Building, she has visited the Statue of Liberty, and she has taken a tour of the United Nations.

However, there's a lot she hasn't done yet. She hasn't gone to a concert, she hasn't spent time at any art museums, and she hasn't gone to the top of the World Trade Center.

Sharon likes New York. She has done a lot of things, and there's still a lot more to do.

✔CHECK-UP

Listening

Sharon is on vacation in San Francisco. She's checking her list of things to do while she's on vacation. On the list below, check the things Sharon has already done.

Alan is a secretary in a very busy office. He's checking his list of things to do before 5 P.M. on Friday. On the list below, check the things Alan has already done.

It's Saturday, and Judy and Paul Johnson are doing lots of things around the house. They're checking the list of things they have to do today. On the list below, check the things they've already done.

____ see the Golden Gate Bridge

____ visit Golden Gate Park

____ take a tour of Alcatraz Prison

____ go to Chinatown

____ eat at Fisherman's Wharf

____ buy souvenirs

____ call Mrs. Porter

____ type the letter to the Ajax Insurance Company

____ go to the bank

____ take the mail to the post office

____ clean the coffee machine

____ speak to the boss about my salary

____ do the laundry

____ wash the kitchen windows

____ pay the bills

____ clean the garage

____ fix the bathroom sink

____ vacuum the living room

✏IN YOUR OWN WORDS

For Writing and Discussion

1. Tell about your experiences in the place where you live.
   What have you done? What haven't you done yet?

2. Make a list of things you usually do at school, at work, or at home. Check the things you've already done this week. Share your list with other students in your class. Tell about what you've done and what you haven't done.

Present Perfect vs. Present Tense
Present Perfect vs. Past Tense
Since/For

A Very Dedicated Doctor

A Wonderful Family

Working Their Way Up to the Top

A VERY DEDICATED DOCTOR

Dr. Fernando's waiting room is very full today. A lot of people are waiting to see him, and they're hoping that the doctor can help them. George's neck has been stiff for more than a week. Martha has had a bad headache since yesterday, and Lenny has felt dizzy since early this morning. Carol has had a high fever for two days, Bob's knee has been swollen for three weeks, Bill's arm has been black and blue since last weekend, and Tommy and Julie have had little red spots all over their bodies for the past twenty-four hours.

Dr. Fernando has been in the office since early this morning. He has already seen a lot of patients, and he will certainly see many more before the day is over. Dr. Fernando's patients don't know it, but he also isn't feeling well. He has had a pain in his back since last Thursday, but he hasn't taken any time to stay at home and rest. He has had a lot of patients this week, and he's a very dedicated doctor.

Q & A

Dr. Fernando's patients are talking to him about their problems. Using this model, create dialogs based on the story.

A. So how are you feeling today, *George?*
B. Not very well, Dr. Fernando.
A. What seems to be the problem?
B. *My neck is stiff.*
A. I see. Tell me, how long *has your neck been stiff?*
B. *For more than a week.*

Choose

1. They've known each other since
    a. 1985.
    b. three years.

2. I've been interested in history for
    a. last year.
    b. one year.

3. She has been a doctor for
    a. two years ago.
    b. two years.

4. I've had a backache since
    a. yesterday.
    b. two days.

5. We've been here for
    a. one hour.
    b. one o'clock.

6. There have been two robberies in our neighborhood since
    a. one month.
    b. last month.

7. My grandparents have owned this house for
    a. a long time.
    b. many years ago.

8. They've been in love since
    a. last spring.
    b. three months.

Choose

1. My right arm has been very
    a. dizzy.
    b. stiff.

2. My son has a high
    a. fever.
    b. pain.

3. How long has your arm been
    a. nauseous?
    b. swollen?

4. Jeff's leg has been black and
    a. blue.
    b. red.

5. I've looked at your X-rays, and I think you have
    a. lungs.
    b. pneumonia.

6. Look! I have spots all over my
    a. measles!
    b. body!

READING

A WONDERFUL FAMILY

Mr. and Mrs. Patterson are very proud of their family. Their daughter, Ruth, is a very successful engineer. She has been an engineer since she finished college. Her husband's name is Pablo. They have been happily married for thirty-five years. Pablo is a professional guitarist. He has known how to play the guitar since he was four years old.

Ruth and Pablo have two children. Their son, David, is a computer programmer. He has been interested in computers since he was a teenager. Their daughter, Rita, is a doctor. She has been a doctor since she finished medical school in 1981.

Mr. and Mrs. Patterson also have a son, Herbert. Herbert is single. He has been a bachelor all his life. He's a famous journalist. They haven't seen him since he moved to Singapore several years ago.

Mr. and Mrs. Patterson feel fortunate to have such wonderful children and grandchildren. They're very proud of them.

✔ CHECK-UP

True or False?

1. Ruth's husband is a professional violinist.
2. Ruth and Pablo have two teenagers.
3. The Pattersons' grandson is interested in computers.
4. Rita has been in medical school since 1981.
5. Herbert has never been married.
6. Herbert hasn't seen his parents since they moved to Singapore several years ago.

Listening

Listen to the conversation and choose the answer that is true.

1. a. He doesn't have a toothache now.
   b. He still has a toothache.

2. a. His knee isn't swollen now.
   b. His knee is still swollen.

3. a. Her father is an engineer.
   b. Her father isn't an engineer.

4. a. She's a teenager.
   b. She isn't a teenager.

5. a. He has lived in Rome for 5 years.
   b. He lived in Rome for 5 years.

6. a. Jim has lived in Greece.
   b. Jim lives in Greece.

7. a. Betty went home 2 days ago.
   b. Betty hasn't been home for 2 days.

8. a. He has lived in Nashville for 7 years.
   b. He lived in Nashville for 7 years.

READING

WORKING THEIR WAY UP TO THE TOP

Louis is very successful. For the past six years, he has been the manager of the Big Value Supermarket on Grant Street. Louis has worked very hard to get where he is today. First, he was a clerk for two years. Then, he was a cashier for three years. After that, he was an assistant manager for five years. Finally, six years ago, he became the manager of the store. Everybody at the Big Value Supermarket is very proud of Louis. He started at the bottom, and he has worked his way up to the top.

Florence is very successful. For the past two years, she has been the president of the Jason Department Store Corporation. Florence has worked very hard to get where she is today. She started her career at the Jason Department Store in Nashville, Tennessee. First, she was a salesperson in the Children's Clothing Department for three years. Then, she was the manager of the Women's Clothing Department for ten years. Then, she was the store manager for eight years. After that, she moved to New York and became a vice-president of the corporation. Finally, two years ago, she became the president. Everybody at the Jason Department Store in Nashville is very proud of Florence. She started at the bottom, and she has worked her way up to the top.

✔CHECK-UP

True, False, or Maybe?

Answer True, False, or Maybe (if the answer isn't in the story).

1. Louis started as a cashier at the Big Value Supermarket.
2. He has worked there for sixteen years.
3. All employees at the Big Value Supermarket start at the bottom.
4. Florence has been the manager of the Women's Clothing Department in Nashville for ten years.
5. The Children's Clothing Department was on the bottom floor of the store.
6. Florence hasn't been a vice-president for two years.

IN YOUR OWN WORDS

For Writing and Discussion

Tell a story about your English teacher.

How long have you know him/her?
How long has he/she been an English teacher?
What did he/she do before that? How long?
Where does he/she live?
How long has he/she lived there?
Has he/she lived anywhere else? Where? How long?
Is he/she married? How long?
Besides teaching English, what is your English teacher interested in?
How long has he/she been interested in that?

Present Perfect Continuous Tense

Apartment Problems

It's Been a Long Day

APARTMENT PROBLEMS

Mr. and Mrs. Banks have been having a lot of problems in their apartment recently. For several weeks their bedroom ceiling has been leaking, their refrigerator hasn't been working, and the paint in their hallway has been peeling. In addition, they have been taking cold showers since last week because their water heater hasn't been working, and they haven't been sleeping at night because their radiators have been making strange noises.

Mr. and Mrs. Banks are furious. They have been calling their landlord every day and complaining about their problems. He has been promising to help them, but they have been waiting for more than a week, and he still hasn't fixed anything at all.

✓ CHECK-UP

Q & A

Mr. and Mrs. Banks are calling their landlord for the first time about each of the problems in their apartment. Using this model, create dialogs based on the story.

A. Hello.
B. Hello. This is *Mrs*. Banks.
A. Yes, *Mrs*. Banks. What can I do for you?
B. We're having a problem with *our bedroom ceiling*.
A. Oh? What's the problem?
B. *It's leaking*.
A. I see. Tell me, how long *has it been leaking*?
B. *It's been leaking for about an hour*.
A. All right, *Mrs*. Banks. I'll take care of it as soon as I can.
B. Thank you.

How about YOU?

Have you been having problems in your apartment or house recently? Tell about some problems you've been having.

READING

IT'S BEEN A LONG DAY

Mario has been assembling cameras since 7 A.M., and he's very tired. He has assembled 19 cameras today, and he has NEVER assembled that many cameras in one day before! He has to assemble only one more camera, and then he can go home. He's really glad. It's been a long day.

Judy has been typing letters since 9 A.M., and she's very tired. She has typed 25 letters today, and she has NEVER typed that many letters in one day before! She has to type only one more letter, and then she can go home. She's really glad. It's been a very long day.

Officers Jackson and Parker have been writing parking tickets since 8 A.M., and they're exhausted! They have written 211 parking tickets today, and they have NEVER written that many parking tickets in one day before! They have to write only one more parking ticket, and then they can go home. They're really glad. It's been an extremely long day.

✔CHECK-UP

Listening

I. Listen and decide who is speaking.

1. a. a landlord   b. a boss
2. a. a teacher   b. a student
3. a. a policeman   b. a movie theater cashier
4. a. a window washer   b. a baby-sitter
5. a. a singer   b. a teacher
6. a. a doctor   b. a bookkeeper

II. Listen and choose the word you hear.

1. a. gone   b. going
2. a. written   b. writing
3. a. seen   b. seeing
4. a. taken   b. taking
5. a. given   b. giving
6. a. driven   b. driving

✏IN YOUR OWN WORDS

Tell about yourself.

Where do you live?
How long have you been living there?
Have you lived anywhere else?
Where? How long?

Where do you work or go to school?
How long have you been working or going to school there?

Have you worked or gone to school anywhere else? Where? How long?
What did you do there?
What did you study?

Now interview a friend, a neighbor, or someone in your family and tell the class about this person.

25

Gerunds
Infinitives

Enjoying Life
Bad Habits
Important Decisions

READING

ENJOYING LIFE

Howard enjoys reading. He likes to read in the park. He likes to read in the library. He even likes to read in the bathtub! As you can see, reading is a very important part of Howard's life.

Patty enjoys singing. She likes to sing in school. She likes to sing in church. She even likes to sing in the shower! As you can see, singing is a very important part of Patty's life.

Brenda enjoys watching TV. She likes to watch TV in the living room. She likes to watch TV in bed. She even likes to watch TV in department stores! As you can see, watching TV is a very important part of Brenda's life.

Tom enjoys talking about politics. He likes to talk about politics with his friends. He likes to talk about politics with his parents. He even likes to talk about politics with his barber! As you can see, talking about politics is a very important part of Tom's life.

✓ CHECK-UP

Q & A

The people in the story are introducing themselves to you at a party. Using this model, create dialogs based on the story.

A. Hello. My name is *Howard*.
B. Nice to meet you, *Howard*. I'm _____.
A. Are you enjoying the party?
B. Yes. How about you?
A. Well, not really. To tell you the truth, I'd rather be *reading*.
B. Oh? Do you like to *read*?
A. Oh, yes. I enjoy *reading* very much. How about you?
B. I like to *read*, too. In fact, *reading* is my favorite way to relax.
A. Mine, too. Tell me, what do you like to *read*?
B. I like to *read books about famous people*. How about you?
A. I enjoy *reading short stories*.
B. Well, please excuse me. I have to go now. It was nice meeting you, *Howard*.
A. Nice meeting you, too, _____.

READING

BAD HABITS

Harriet's friends always tell her to stop smoking. They think that smoking is unhealthy. Harriet knows that, but she still keeps on smoking. She wants to stop, but she can't. Smoking is a habit she just can't break.

Vincent's friends always tell him to stop gossiping. They think that gossiping isn't nice. Vincent knows that, but he still keeps on gossiping. He wants to stop, but he can't. Gossiping is a habit he just can't break.

Jennifer's mother always tells her to stop interrupting people while they're talking. She thinks that interrupting people is very rude. Jennifer knows that, but she still keeps on interrupting people. She wants to stop, but she can't. Interrupting people is a habit she just can't break.

Walter's wife always tells him to stop talking about business all the time. She thinks that talking about business all the time is boring. Walter knows that, but he still keeps on talking about business. He wants to stop, but he can't. Talking about business is a habit he just can't break.

✔ CHECK-UP

Q & A

You're talking with the people in this story about their bad habits. Using this model, create dialogs based on the story.

A. *Harriet?*
B. Yes?
A. You know . . . I don't mean to be critical, but I really think you should stop *smoking*.
B. Oh?
A. Yes. *Smoking is unhealthy.* Don't you think so?
B. You're right. The truth is . . . I want to stop, but I can't. *Smoking* is a habit I just can't break.

Do you have any habits you "just can't break"?
Tell about them.

IMPORTANT DECISIONS

Jim had to make an important decision recently. He made an appointment for an interview at the Acme Insurance Company, and he had to decide what to wear. First, he considered wearing a sweater to the interview. Then, he thought about wearing a sports jacket. Finally, he decided to wear a suit and tie. Jim thinks he made the right decision. He's glad he didn't wear a sweater or sports jacket. He feels that wearing a suit and tie was the best thing for him to do.

Lana had to make an important decision recently. Her landlord sold her apartment building, and she had to decide where to move. First, she considered moving to another apartment. Then, she thought about buying a small house. Finally, she decided to move home with her parents for a while. Lana thinks she made the right decision. She's glad she didn't move to another apartment or buy a small house. She feels that moving home with her parents for a while was the right thing for her to do.

Nick had to make an important decision recently. He got out of the army, and he had to decide what to do next with his life. First, he considered working in his family's grocery store. Then, he thought about taking a job in a restaurant. Finally, he decided to enroll in college and study engineering. Nick thinks he made the right decision. He's glad he didn't work in his family's grocery store or take a job in a restaurant. He feels that enrolling in college and studying engineering was the smartest thing for him to do.

Maria had to make an important decision recently. She lost her job as a bookkeeper because her company went out of business, and she had to decide what to do. First, she considered looking for another job as a bookkeeper. Then, she thought about working as a secretary for a while. Finally, she decided to enroll in technical school and study computer programming. Maria thinks she made the right decision. She's glad she didn't look for another job as a bookkeeper or work as a secretary for a while. She feels that enrolling in technical school and studying computer programming was the best thing for her to do.

✔ CHECK-UP

True, False, or Maybe?

Answer True, False, or Maybe (if the answer isn't in the story).

1. Jim considered wearing a sweater to the interview.
2. He got the job at the Acme Insurance Company.
3. Lana decided not to move to another apartment.
4. Lana never considered buying a small house.
5. Lana's parents think that moving home was the right thing for Lana to do.
6. Nick's family is in the restaurant business.
7. Nick first became interested in engineering while he was in the army.
8. Maria wasn't a very good bookkeeper.
9. After Maria lost her job, she worked as a secretary for a while.
10. Maria feels she made the right decision.

Q & A

The people in the story are asking you for advice about the decisions they have to make. Using this model, create dialogs based on the story.

A. Can I ask you a question?
B. Sure.
A. I need some advice. *I've* just *made an appointment for a job interview at the Acme Insurance Company*, and now I have to decide *what to wear*.
B. Hmm. That's an important decision.
A. It is. I've considered *wearing a sweater*. I've also been thinking about *wearing a sports jacket*. But I'm not really sure. What do you think?
B. Well . . . Have you considered *wearing a suit and tie*?
A. No. That's a good idea. I'll think about it. Thanks.

Choose

I.
1. Can you ____ me how?
   a. practice
   b. teach

2. Playing chess is my ____ way to relax.
   a. enjoy
   b. favorite

3. Gossiping is a bad ____.
   a. habit
   b. rude

4. I'm not sure what to do. Do you have any good ____?
   a. decisions
   b. suggestions

5. I ____ you.
   a. enroll
   b. envy

6. Please don't ____ our conversation.
   a. interrupt
   b. break

II.
1. My sister ____ traveling by train.
   a. likes to
   b. enjoys

2. Jimmy ____ to do his homework.
   a. avoids
   b. can't stand

3. I've ____ to go on a diet.
   a. decided
   b. considered

4. I ____ swim when I was three years old.
   a. began
   b. started to

5. ____ is an important decision.
   a. Buying a house
   b. Buy a house

6. I know I shouldn't ____ eat junk food.
   a. continue to
   b. keep on

Listening

Listen and choose the best answer.

1. a. He enjoys driving downtown.
   b. He hates driving downtown.

2. a. She sold her car.
   b. She's going to sell her car.

3. a. He bites his nails.
   b. He stopped biting his nails.

4. a. They're going to move to California.
   b. They might move to California.

5. a. He's married.
   b. He isn't married.

6. a. She's going to keep on practicing.
   b. She isn't going to continue practicing.

IN YOUR OWN WORDS

For Writing and Discussion

AN IMPORTANT DECISION

Tell a story about an important decision you had to make.

I had to make an important decision recently.
_____, and I
had to decide what to do. First, I considered
_____. Then, I thought about _____.
Finally, I decided to _____. I'm glad I didn't
_____ or _____. I feel that
_____ was the best thing for me to do.

8

Past Perfect Tense
Past Perfect Continuous Tense

The Most Important Thing

Days Gone By

Nobody Was Surprised

THE MOST IMPORTANT THING

Roger thought he was all prepared for his dinner party last night. He had sent invitations to his boss and all the people at the office. He had looked through several cookbooks and had found some very interesting recipes. He had even gone all the way downtown to buy imported fruit, vegetables, and cheese, which he needed for his dinner. However, as soon as Roger's doorbell rang and his guests arrived, he realized that he had forgotten to turn on the oven. Roger felt very foolish. He couldn't believe what he had done. He thought he was all prepared for his dinner party, but he had forgotten to do the most important thing.

Mr. and Mrs. Jenkins thought they were all prepared for their vacation. They had packed their suitcases several days ahead of time. They had gone to the bank and purchased travelers checks. They had even asked their next-door neighbor to water their plants, feed their dog, and shovel their driveway in case it snowed. However, as soon as Mr. and Mrs. Jenkins arrived at the airport, they realized that they had forgotten to bring their plane tickets with them, and there wasn't enough time to go back home and get them. Mr. and Mrs. Jenkins were heartbroken. They couldn't believe what they had done. They thought they were all prepared for their vacation, but they had forgotten to do the most important thing.

Harold thought he was all prepared for his job interview yesterday. He had gone to his barber and gotten a very short haircut. He had bought a new shirt, put on his best tie, and shined his shoes. He had even borrowed his brother's new suit. However, as soon as Harold began the job interview, he realized that he had forgotten to bring along his resume. Harold was furious with himself. He thought he was all prepared for his job interview, but he had forgotten to do the most important thing.

Janet thought she was all prepared for the school play. She had memorized the script several weeks in advance. She had practiced her songs and dances until she knew them perfectly. She had even stayed up all night the night before and rehearsed the play by herself from beginning to end. However, as soon as the curtain went up and the play began last night, Janet realized that she had forgotten to put on her costume. Janet was really embarrassed. She couldn't believe what she had done. She thought she was all prepared for the play, but she had forgotten to do the most important thing.

✓ CHECK-UP

True, False, or Maybe?

Answer True, False, or Maybe (if the answer isn't in the story).

1. Roger hadn't remembered to cook the food.
2. Roger's guests couldn't believe what he had done.
3. Mr. and Mrs. Jenkins had forgotten to buy their plane tickets.
4. When Mr. and Mrs. Jenkins realized what had happened, they felt very sad and upset.
5. Harold thinks it's important to bring a resume to a job interview.
6. Harold doesn't have a suit.
7. Janet hadn't seen the script until the night before the play.
8. Before the play began, Janet hadn't realized that she had forgotten to put on her costume.

Choose

1. Before Barbara went on her vacation, she went to the bank and bought

   | tickets |
   | travelers checks |

2. Peter wanted his boss to come over for dinner, but he forgot to send him

   | a resume |
   | an invitation |

3. Sheila

   | borrowed |
   | bought |

   her roommate's typewriter for a few days.

4. Our grandchildren were

   | heartbroken |
   | foolish |

   when our dog ran away.

5. At the supermarket next to the United Nations,

   | imported |
   | important |

   people buy

   | imported |
   | important |

   food.

How about YOU?

Have you ever thought you were all prepared for something, but then you realized you had forgotten to do something important?
What were you preparing for?
What had you done?
What had you forgotten to do?

DAYS GONE BY

Michael took a very special trip last month. He went back to Fullerton, his home town. Michael's visit to Fullerton was very special to him. He was born there, he grew up there, but he hadn't been back there since he finished high school.

He went to places he hadn't gone to in years. He walked through the park in the center of town and remembered the days he had walked through that same park with his first girlfriend. He passed by the empty field where he and his friends had played baseball every day after school. And he stood for a while in front of the movie theater and thought about all the Saturday afternoons he had spent there sitting in the balcony, watching his favorite movie heroes and eating popcorn.

He did things he hadn't done in a long time. He had some homemade ice cream at the ice cream shop, he rode on the merry-go-round in the park, and he went fishing at the lake on the outskirts of town. For a little while, he felt like a kid again. He hadn't had homemade ice cream, ridden on a merry-go-round, or gone fishing since he was a young boy.

He also saw people he hadn't seen in years. He visited several of his old neighbors who had never moved out of the neighborhood. He said hello to the owners of the candy store near his house. And he even bumped into Mrs. Riley, his tenth-grade science teacher!

During his visit to his home town, Michael remembered places he hadn't gone to, things he hadn't done, and people he hadn't seen since his childhood. Michael's trip back to Fullerton was a very nostalgic experience for him. Going back to Fullerton brought back many memories of days gone by.

True, False, or Maybe?

Answer True, False, or Maybe (if the answer isn't in the story).

1. Michael moved back to Fullerton last month.
2. He hadn't seen Fullerton in years.
3. When Michael passed by the field last month, children were playing baseball.
4. Michael enjoyed going to the movies when he was young.
5. The ice cream shop was near Michael's home in Fullerton.
6. Michael rode on the merry-go-round when he was a young boy.
7. Some of Michael's old neighbors still live in the same neighborhood.
8. Mrs. Riley still teaches science.

Choose

What word doesn't belong?

1. a. river   b. ocean   c. park   d. lake
2. a. evening   b. before   c. weekend   d. week
3. a. movies   b. candy   c. ice cream d. popcorn
4. a. end   b. finish   c. close   d. start
5. a. resume   b. invitation c. interview d. script
6. a. prepare   b. rehearse   c. realize   d. memorize

Listening

Listen and choose the best answer.

1. a. Did you like it?
   b. When are you going to see it?

2. a. Did you enjoy it?
   b. Why not?

3. a. It had already started.
   b. It has already begun.

4. a. But I had already done it.
   b. But I've already done it.

5. a. She had memorized all the important names and dates.
   b. She's going to study very hard.

6. a. Had you ever eaten there before?
   b. Have you ever eaten there?

How about YOU?

Tell about feelings you have had.

I feel nostalgic when . . . .
I felt foolish when . . . .
I was furious when . . . .
I was heartbroken when . . . .

NOBODY WAS SURPRISED

When Stella Karp won the marathon last week, nobody was surprised. She had been getting up early and jogging every morning. She had been eating health foods and taking vitamins for several months. And she had been swimming fifty laps every day after work. Stella Karp really deserved to win the marathon. After all, she had been preparing for it for a long time.

When my friend Stuart finally passed his driver's test the other day, nobody was surprised. He had been taking lessons at the driving school for several months. He had been practicing driving with his father for the past several weeks. And he had been studying the "rules of the road" in the driver's manual since he was a little boy. My friend Stuart really deserved to pass his driver's test. After all, he had been preparing for it for a long time.

When Sally Compton got a promotion last week, nobody was surprised. She had been working overtime every day for several months. She had been studying computer programming in the evening. And she had even been taking extra work home on the weekends. Sally Compton really deserved to get a promotion. After all, she had been working hard to earn it for a long time.

IN YOUR OWN WORDS

For Writing and Discussion

We shouldn't be surprised when we accomplish something that we have worked for. Tell a story about something you accomplished.

What did you accomplish?
How long had you been preparing for that?
How had you been preparing?

9

Two-Word Verbs:
Separable
Inseparable

A Busy Saturday

Lucy's English Composition

A Child-Rearing Problem

On Sale

READING

A BUSY SATURDAY

Everybody in the Martini family is very busy today. It's Saturday, and they all have to do the things they didn't do during the week.

Mr. Martini has to fill out his income tax form. He didn't have time to fill it out during the week.

Mrs. Martini has to pick up her clothes at the cleaner's. She was too busy to pick them up during the week.

Their son Frank has to throw out all the old magazines and newspapers in the garage. He didn't have time to throw them out during the week.

Their other son, Bob, has to take his library books back. He forgot to take them back during the week.

And their daughter, Julie, has to put her toys away. She didn't feel like putting them away during the week.

As you can see, everybody in the Martini family is going to be very busy today.

✓CHECK-UP

Q & A

You're inviting somebody in the Martini family to do something with you. Using this model, create dialogs based on the story.

A. Would you like to *go fishing* this morning?
B. I'd like to, but I can't. I have to *fill out my income tax form*.
A. That's too bad.
B. I know, but I've really got to do it. I *didn't have time to fill it out* during the week.
A. Well, maybe some other time.
B. Okay.

How about YOU?

What do you have to do on your next day off from work or school?

READING

LUCY'S ENGLISH COMPOSITION

Lucy is very discouraged. She handed in her English composition this morning, but her English teacher gave it right back to her and told her to do it over. Apparently, her English teacher didn't like the way she had done it. She hadn't erased her mistakes. She had simply crossed them out. Also, she had used several words incorrectly, since she hadn't looked them up in the dictionary. And finally, she hadn't written her homework on the correct paper because she had accidentally thrown her notebook away. Poor Lucy! She didn't feel like writing her English composition in the first place, and now she has to do it over!

✓CHECK-UP

What's the Word?

Choose the correct words to complete the sentences.

do over	give back	hand in	look up	throw away

1. I need the dictionary you borrowed from me. Please _____ _____ _____ .
2. I want to check your homework. Please _____ _____ _____ .
3. Ms. Smith, there are too many mistakes in this letter. Please _____ _____ _____ .
4. I haven't read today's newspaper yet. Please don't _____ _____ _____ .
5. I don't remember his phone number. Please _____ _____ _____ .

Listening: *DEAR ALICE*

Listen and write the missing words.

Dear Alice,

   I'm very discouraged. I'm having a lot of trouble with my girlfriend, and I don't know what to do. The problem is very simple. I'm in love with her, but she isn't in love with me! A few weeks ago I gave her a ring, but she _____.[1] During the past few months I have written several love letters to her, but she has _____.[2] Recently I asked her to marry me. She _____[3] for a while, and then she _____.[4] Now when I try to _____[5] she doesn't even want to talk to me. Please try to help me. I don't know what to do.

"Discouraged Donald"
Denver, Colorado

What should "Discouraged Donald" do?   Write an answer to his letter.

A CHILD-REARING PROBLEM

Timmy and his little sister, Patty, don't get along with each other very well. In fact, they fight constantly. He picks on her when it's time for her to go to bed. She picks on him when his friends come over to play.

Timmy and Patty's parents are very concerned. They don't know what to do about their children. They have looked through several books on child rearing, but so far they can't seem to find an answer to the problem. They're hoping that eventually their children will learn to get along better with each other.

✔CHECK-UP

True, False, or Maybe?

Answer True, False, or Maybe (if the answer isn't in the story).

1. Patty picks on Timmy when it's time for her to go to bed.
2. Timmy is Patty's older brother.
3. Timmy and Patty's parents have a child-rearing problem.
4. They can't seem to find any books about child rearing.
5. Timmy and Patty will eventually learn to get along better with each other.

Choose

1. Please don't ____ your little sister.
   a. pick on
   b. get along with

2. We've been ____ these old family pictures.
   a. looking through
   b. taking after

3. My teacher ____ me three times today.
   a. looked up to
   b. called on

4. I haven't ____ my aunt and uncle recently.
   a. gotten over
   b. heard from

5. I really ____ my older sister because she's so smart.
   a. run into
   b. look up to

6. Everybody thinks I ____ my mother.
   a. look through
   b. take after

7. I ____ my cousin Betty on Main Street yesterday.
   a. ran into
   b. heard from

8. Don't kiss me! I haven't ____ my cold yet.
   a. gotten along with
   b. gotten over

ON SALE

Melvin went to a men's clothing store yesterday. He was looking for a new sports jacket. He looked through the entire selection of jackets and picked out a few that he really liked. First, he picked out a nice blue jacket. But when he tried it on, it was too small. Next, he picked out an attractive red jacket. But when he tried it on, it was too large. Finally, he picked out a very fancy brown jacket with gold buttons. And when he tried it on, it seemed to fit perfectly.

Then he decided to buy a pair of trousers to go with the jacket. He looked through the entire selection of trousers and picked out several pairs that he really liked. First, he picked out a light brown pair. But when he tried them on, they were too tight. Next, he picked out a dark brown pair. But when he tried them on, they were too loose. Finally, he picked out a pair of brown-and-white plaid pants. And when he tried them on, they seemed to fit perfectly.

Melvin paid for his new clothing and walked home feeling very happy about the jacket and pants he had just bought. He was especially happy because the clothing was on sale and he had paid 50 percent off the regular price.

However, Melvin's happiness didn't last very long. When he got home, he noticed that one arm of the jacket was longer than the other. He also realized very quickly that the zipper on the pants was broken.

The next day Melvin took the clothing back to the store and tried to get a refund. However, the people at the store refused to give him his money back because the clothing was on sale and there was a sign that said "ALL SALES ARE FINAL!"

Melvin was furious, but he knew he couldn't do anything about it. The next time he buys something on sale, he'll be more careful. And he'll be sure to read the signs!

✓ CHECK-UP

What's the Sequence?

Put these sentences in the correct order, based on the story.

_____ But then, Melvin noticed problems with the jacket and the pants.
_____ Melvin picked out a few jackets he really liked.
_____ Melvin went back and asked for a refund.
_1_ Melvin went shopping for clothes yesterday.
_____ He walked home feeling very happy.
_____ He walked home feeling very upset and angry.
_____ The brown jacket seemed to fit perfectly.
_____ The store refused to give him back his money.
_____ A pair of plaid pants fit very well.
_____ He paid only half of the regular price.
_____ He picked out several pairs of trousers.

Listening

Listen and choose what the people are talking about.

1. a. an application form
   b. a math problem

2. a. shorts
   b. a blouse

3. a. shoes
   b. library books

4. a. homework
   b. children

5. a. pictures
   b. pants

6. a. the flu
   b. a decision

7. a. a coat
   b. the heat

8. a. milk
   b. the garbage

✏ IN YOUR OWN WORDS

For Writing and Discussion

Have you ever bought anything that you had to return? Tell about it.

What did you buy?
Where?
What was wrong with it?
What did you do?
Were you successful?

■ 44

Connectors:
And . . . Too
And . . . Either
So, But, Neither

Made for Each Other

Laid Off

Touchy Subjects

MADE FOR EACH OTHER

Louise and Brian are very compatible people. They have a lot in common. For example, they have very similar backgrounds. He grew up in a small town in the South, and so did she. She's the oldest of four children, and he is, too. His parents own their own business, and so do hers.

They also have similar academic interests. She's majoring in Chemistry, and he is, too. He has taken every course in Mathematics offered by their college, and so has she. She enjoys working with computers, and he does, too.

In addition, Louise and Brian like the same sports. He goes swimming several times a week, and so does she. She can play tennis very well, and so can he. His favorite winter sport is ice skating, and hers is, too.

Louise and Brian also have the same cultural interests. She has been to most of the art museums in New York City, and so has he. He's a member of the college theater group, and she is, too. She has a complete collection of Beethoven's symphonies, and so does he.

In addition, they have very similar personalities. She has always been very shy, and he has, too. He tends to be very quiet, and so does she. She's often nervous when she's in large groups of people, and he is, too.

Finally, they have very similar outlooks on life. She has been a vegetarian for years, and so has he. He supports equal rights for women and minorities, and so does she. She's opposed to the use of nuclear energy, and he is, too.

As you can see, Louise and Brian are very compatible people. In fact, everybody says they were "made for each other."

✔ CHECK-UP

True, False, or Maybe?

Answer True, False, or Maybe (if the answer isn't in the story).

1. Brian doesn't have any older brothers or sisters.
2. Louise and Brian are both students in college.
3. They both ski very well.
4. They haven't been to all the art museums in New York City.
5. They both feel that people shouldn't eat vegetables.

Listening

Listen and choose what the people are talking about.

1. a. personality
   b. background

2. a. sports
   b. cultural interests

3. a. academic interests
   b. outlook on life

4. a. personality
   b. background

5. a. cultural interests
   b. outlook on life

READING

LAID OFF

Jack and Betty Williams are going through some difficult times. They were both laid off from their jobs last month. As the days go by, they're becoming more and more concerned about their futures, since he hasn't been able to find another job yet, and neither has she.

The layoffs weren't a surprise to Jack and Betty. After all, Jack's company hadn't been doing very well for a long time, and neither had Betty's. However, Jack had never expected both of them to be laid off at the same time, and Betty hadn't either. Ever since they have been laid off, Jack and Betty have been trying to find new jobs. Unfortunately, she hasn't been very successful, and he hasn't either.

The main reason they're having trouble finding work is that there simply aren't many jobs available right now. He can't find anything in the want ads, and neither can she. She hasn't heard about any job openings, and he hasn't either. His friends haven't been able to help at all, and neither have hers.

Another reason they're having trouble finding work is that they don't seem to have the right kind of skills and training. He doesn't know anything about computers, and she doesn't either. She can't type very well, and neither can he. He hasn't had any special vocational training, and she hasn't either.

A third reason they're having trouble finding work is that there are certain jobs they prefer not to take. He doesn't like working at night, and neither does she. She isn't willing to work on the weekends, and neither is he. He doesn't want to commute very far to work, and she doesn't either.

Despite all their problems, Jack and Betty aren't completely discouraged. She doesn't have a very pessimistic outlook on life, and neither does he. They're both hopeful that things will get better soon.

CHECK-UP

True, False, or Maybe?

Answer True, False, or Maybe (if the answer isn't in the story).

1. Jack quit his job last month.
2. Jack and Betty had been working for the same company.
3. Some of their friends have been laid off, too.
4. Typing skills are important in certain jobs.
5. Jack and Betty will find jobs soon.

A Job Interview

You're at a job interview. Role play with another student, using the interviewer's questions below.

Tell me about your skills.
Tell me about your educational background.
Have you had any special vocational training?
Are you willing to work at night or on weekends?
When can you start?

READING

TOUCHY SUBJECTS

Larry and his parents never agree when they talk about politics. Larry is very liberal, but his parents aren't. They're very conservative. Larry thinks the President is doing a very poor job, but his parents don't. They think the President is doing a fine job. Also, Larry doesn't think the government should spend a lot of money on defense, but his parents do. They think the country needs a strong army. You can see why Larry and his parents never agree when they talk about politics. Politics is a very "touchy subject" with them.

The Greens and their next-door neighbors, the Harrisons, never agree when they talk about child rearing. The Greens are very lenient with their children, but the Harrisons aren't. They're very strict. The Greens let their children watch television whenever they want, but the Harrisons don't. They let their children watch television for only an hour a day. Also, the Harrisons have always taught their children to sit quietly and behave well at the dinner table, but the Greens haven't. They have always allowed their children to do whatever they want at the dinner table. You can see why the Greens and their next-door neighbors, the Harrisons, never agree when they talk about child rearing. Child rearing is a very "touchy subject" with them.

✔ CHECK-UP

True or False?

1. Larry and his parents always disagree when they talk about politics.
2. Larry probably supports equal rights for women and minorities.
3. The Harrisons' children watch television more often than the Greens' children.
4. The Greens' children probably go to bed later than the Harrisons' children.
5. Since the Greens and the Harrisons disagree, they never talk about child rearing.

IN YOUR OWN WORDS

For Writing and Discussion

Tell a story about a "touchy subject" between you and another person.

Who is the person?
What do you disagree about?
In what ways do you disagree?
(Use "I _____, but _____" in your story.)

Passive Voice

Alan Almost Didn't Get to Work This Morning

A Very Exciting Year

Joe's Auto Repair Shop

A National Historic Landmark

ALAN ALMOST DIDN'T GET TO WORK THIS MORNING

Alan almost didn't get to work this morning.

As he was leaving his apartment building, he was hit on the head with a flowerpot which had been put on a windowsill by one of his neighbors.

As he was walking to the bus stop, he was bitten by a dog and stung by a bee.

While he was waiting for the bus, he was almost run over by a car.

While he was riding on the bus, his wallet was stolen. All his money and identification cards were taken.

As he was walking into his office building, he was accidentally knocked down by a boy delivering newspapers.

And when Alan finally got to work, he was yelled at by his boss for being an hour late.

Poor Alan! What a way to begin the day!

 ## CHECK-UP

True, False, or Maybe?

Answer True, False, or Maybe (if the answer isn't in the story).

1. As Alan was leaving his apartment building, one of his neighbors hit him on the head.
2. As he was walking to the bus stop, a dog bit him and a bee stung him.
3. A car almost hit Alan.

4. Alan had a lot of money in his wallet.
5. Alan accidentally knocked down a boy delivering newspapers.
6. Alan was yelled at because he wasn't on time for work.

How about YOU?

Have you ever had a bad day when everything went wrong? What happened? When? How did you feel?

A VERY EXCITING YEAR

In January Martha was hired by the Fernwood Company as a secretary. In March she was sent to school by the company to study statistics and accounting. In April she was given a raise. Just two months later, she was promoted to the position of supervisor of her department.

In August she was chosen "Employee of the Month." In October she was given another raise. In November she was invited to apply for a position in the company's overseas office in Bangkok. And in December she was given the new job and flown to Thailand to begin work.

Martha certainly has had a very exciting year. She can't believe all the wonderful things that have happened to her since she was hired just twelve months ago.

✔ CHECK-UP

Choose

1. The interviewer liked my resume, so I was given the ____.
   a. raise
   b. position

2. After Ted had worked at the company for two years, he was ____.
   a. promoted
   b. hired

3. I was sent overseas ____ my company.
   a. by
   b. as

4. Over one hundred people have ____ the new position.
   a. been invited to
   b. applied for

5. Last month Sarah was ____ a new position in the Accounting Department.
   a. chosen
   b. given

6. I have to type this myself. The new secretary hasn't been ____ yet.
   a. hired
   b. fired

Tell about things that have happened in your life during the past twelve months.

READING

JOE'S AUTO REPAIR SHOP

Wilma Jones has been having a lot of trouble with her car recently, so she decided to take it to Joe's Auto Repair Shop to be fixed. The car is there now and is receiving a LOT of attention from Joe and the other mechanics at his shop.

The engine is being tuned. The oil is being changed. The battery is being charged. The brakes are being adjusted. The heater is being repaired. The broken headlight is being replaced. The hood is being repainted. The tires are being checked. And the broken rear window is being fixed.

Wilma is aware that she's probably going to be charged a lot of money for these repairs. But she's confident that her car will be returned to her in excellent condition by the fine people who work at Joe's Auto Repair Shop.

✓ CHECK-UP

Q & A

Wilma Jones is calling Joe's Auto Repair Shop to find out about her car. Using this model, make questions and answers based on the story.

A. Have you *tuned the engine* yet?
B. No, not yet. *It's* being *tuned* right now.

Listening

Listen and choose the best line to continue the conversation.

1. a. Do you want me to do them?
   b. Who did them?

2. a. Do you want me to send them?
   b. Who sent them?

3. a. Was your cat hurt badly?
   b. Was your dog hurt badly?

4. a. Is she going to go?
   b. Is he going to go?

5. a. When will Mrs. Brown begin working?
   b. When will Mr. Simon begin working?

6. a. When will Mrs. Davis start her new job?
   b. When will Mrs. Clark start her new job?

7. a. Oh, good. I'll pick it up in an hour.
   b. Oh, good. Call me when it's been fixed.

8. a. Oh, good. I'll pick it up right now.
   b. Oh, good. I'll pick it up when it's ready.

54

A NATIONAL HISTORIC LANDMARK

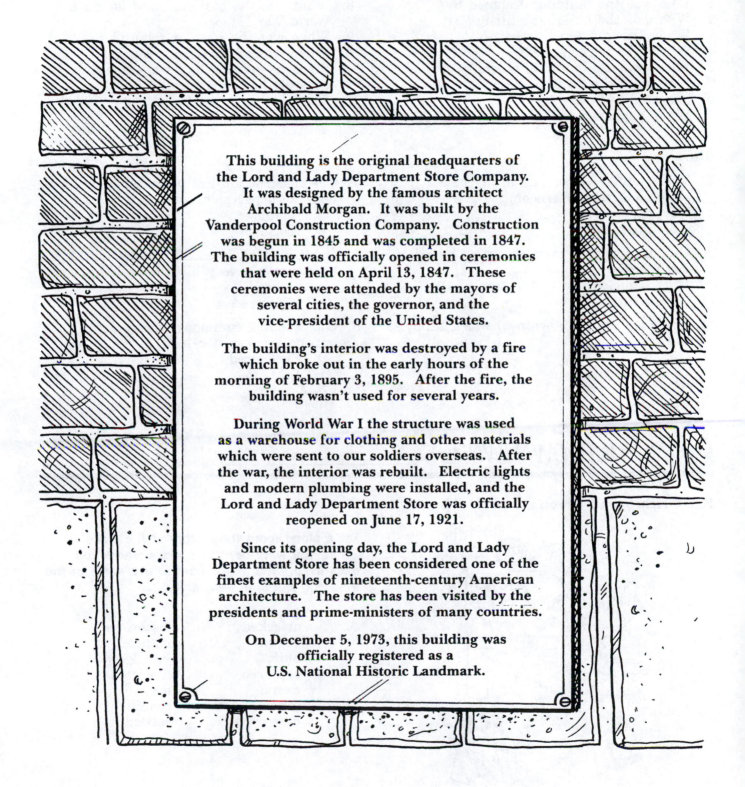

This building is the original headquarters of the Lord and Lady Department Store Company. It was designed by the famous architect Archibald Morgan. It was built by the Vanderpool Construction Company. Construction was begun in 1845 and was completed in 1847. The building was officially opened in ceremonies that were held on April 13, 1847. These ceremonies were attended by the mayors of several cities, the governor, and the vice-president of the United States.

The building's interior was destroyed by a fire which broke out in the early hours of the morning of February 3, 1895. After the fire, the building wasn't used for several years.

During World War I the structure was used as a warehouse for clothing and other materials which were sent to our soldiers overseas. After the war, the interior was rebuilt. Electric lights and modern plumbing were installed, and the Lord and Lady Department Store was officially reopened on June 17, 1921.

Since its opening day, the Lord and Lady Department Store has been considered one of the finest examples of nineteenth-century American architecture. The store has been visited by the presidents and prime-ministers of many countries.

On December 5, 1973, this building was officially registered as a U.S. National Historic Landmark.

Answer These Questions

1. Who was the building designed by?
2. Who was the building built by?
3. When was construction begun?
4. When was it completed?
5. When was the building officially opened?
6. Who were the opening ceremonies attended by?
7. What happened on February 3, 1895?
8. What was the building used for during World War I?
9. When was the interior rebuilt?
10. When was the building reopened?
11. Since its opening day, what has the building been considered?
12. What happened on December 5, 1973?

Choose

1. The telephone was _____ in my new apartment this afternoon.
   a. opened
   b. installed

2. Our anniversary party was _____ by all of our friends.
   a. attended
   b. visited

3. The shoe factory downtown was _____ by the fire.
   a. rebuilt
   b. destroyed

4. The construction has been completed, and now the department store can be _____.
   a. rebuilt
   b. reopened

5. Our City Hall is _____ by many tourists because it's a very historic building.
   a. visited
   b. registered

6. Our wedding ceremony wasn't _____ outside because it rained.
   a. considered
   b. held

✎ IN YOUR OWN WORDS

For Writing and Discussion

Tell a story about the history of the place where you were born or a place where you have lived. You might want to use some of the following words in your story:

attacked	discovered
begun	founded
built	invaded
captured	liberated
closed	opened
conquered	rebuilt
destroyed	settled

12

Noun/Adjective/Adverb Review:
Count/Non-Count Nouns
Comparative of Adjectives
Superlative of Adjectives
Comparative of Adverbs

A Memo from the Boss

Better Than Before

The Seaside Resort Hotel

A MEMO FROM THE BOSS

INTEROFFICE MEMORANDUM

To: All Personnel
From: Mr. Davis
Subject: Use of Office Supplies

I'm very concerned about the use of office supplies. During the past year we have been using too many paper clips, too much paper, too many rubber bands, too much ink, too much typing paper, too many envelopes, and too many pens and pencils.

Beginning immediately, I'd like all of you to use fewer paper clips, less paper, fewer rubber bands, less ink, less typing paper, fewer envelopes, and fewer pens and pencils.

Thank you for your cooperation.

CHECK-UP

Q & A

You're an employee in this office. Mr. Davis is talking with you about your use of office supplies. Using this model, create dialogs based on the memo above.

A. *Howard?*
B. Yes, Mr. Davis?
A. *How many paper clips* have you used today?
B. Not *too many* . . . just *a few*.
A. Good. We've been using *too many paper clips* in this office lately.
B. I know. I read your memo. We're all trying to use *fewer paper clips* these days.
A. Good. I'm glad to hear that. Thank you, *Howard*.
B. You're welcome, Mr. Davis.

READING

BETTER THAN BEFORE

Ronald recently completed a public-speaking class, and he's very pleased with the results. His family has noticed that he's speaking louder, more clearly, and more confidently than before. His boss has noticed that he's more effective in his work. All his friends tell him that he's friendlier and more outgoing than before. And Ronald himself has noticed that he's more comfortable when he speaks with people and he's even enjoying himself more at parties. Ronald is feeling much better about himself these days. That's why he's now recommending the public-speaking class to everybody he knows.

Mr. and Mrs. Peterson recently completed an aerobics class, and they're very pleased with the results. Their children have noticed that they're happier than before. Their friends have noticed that they're looking slimmer and more physically fit than before. All their neighbors tell them that they're more relaxed than before. And Mr. and Mrs. Peterson themselves have noticed that they're more energetic than before. Mr. and Mrs. Peterson are feeling much better about themselves these days. That's why they're now recommending the aerobics class to everybody they know.

Fido recently completed a dog obedience class, and he's very pleased with the results. The other dogs in the neighborhood have noticed that he looks much healthier and prouder than before. The mailman has noticed that he runs faster and jumps higher than before. His family tells him that he rolls over, "plays dead," and does other tricks better than before. And Fido himself has noticed that he feels stronger and looks more handsome than before. Fido is feeling much better about himself these days. That's why he's now recommending the dog obedience class to everybody he knows.

✔ CHECK-UP

True or False?

1. Ronald is studying public speaking now.
2. Ronald used to speak softer.
3. Mr. and Mrs. Peterson were heavier before.
4. They aren't as energetic as they used to be.
5. Fido didn't do tricks before.

Listening

Listen and choose what the people are talking about.

1. a. public-speaking class   b. yoga class
2. a. the mailman   b. the dog
3. a. bicycles   b. employees
4. a. paper   b. rubber bands
5. a. a garden   b. a cake

COME TO THE
Seaside Resort Hotel!

Enjoy our
- clean and beautiful beach!
- clear and warm ocean water!
- spacious and comfortable rooms!
- delicious food!
- friendly and helpful hotel staff!
- challenging golf course!
- entertaining nightclub show!

Come and stay with us!
We promise you'll have a wonderful vacation by the sea!
SEASIDE RESORT HOTEL
SUNNYVILLE, FLORIDA

THE SEASIDE RESORT HOTEL

Shirley and Joe took a vacation last month at the Seaside Resort Hotel. They were very pleased with the hotel and had a wonderful time on their vacation.

The beach was the cleanest and most beautiful they had ever seen. The ocean water was the clearest and warmest they had ever swum in. Their room was the most spacious and most comfortable they had ever stayed in. The food was the most delicious they had ever eaten. The hotel staff was the friendliest and most helpful they had ever encountered. The golf course was the most challenging they had ever played on. And the nightclub show was the most entertaining they had ever been to.

Shirley and Joe really enjoyed themselves at the Seaside Resort Hotel. It was the best vacation they had ever taken.

IN YOUR OWN WORDS

For Writing and Discussion

Come to the
Mountain View RESORT HOTEL

- Stay in our attractive and modern rooms!
- See our scenic mountain views!
- Breathe our fresh mountain air!
- Ski on our challenging ski slopes!
- Skate on our large skating rink!
- Swim in our beautiful indoor pool!
- Dance in our lively discotheque!

Come and stay with us!
We promise you'll have a wonderful vacation in the mountains!
MOUNTAIN VIEW RESORT HOTEL
SNOWVILLE, COLORADO

THE MOUNTAIN VIEW RESORT HOTEL

You took a vacation recently at the Mountain View Resort Hotel, and you had a wonderful time! Using the story above as a guide, tell about your vacation.

Embedded Questions

Rosemary Smith Was Robbed
A "Surprise" Quiz
At the Midtown Medical Clinic

ROSEMARY SMITH WAS ROBBED

Rosemary Smith was robbed about an hour ago while she was walking home from work. She's at the police station now, and she's having a lot of trouble giving the police information. She knows that a man robbed her about an hour ago, but she simply can't remember any of the details.

She has forgotten how tall the man was. She isn't sure how heavy he was. She can't remember what color hair he had. She has no idea what color eyes he had. She doesn't remember what he was wearing. She doesn't know what kind of car he was driving. She can't remember what color the car was. She has no idea what the license number was. And she doesn't even know how much money was taken!

Poor Rosemary! The police want to help her, but she can't remember any of the details.

✔ CHECK-UP

Q & A

You're a police officer. You're trying to get information from Rosemary Smith about the robbery. Using this model, make questions and answers based on the story.

A. Can you tell me* *how tall the man was*?

B. I'm sorry. *I've forgotten how tall he was.*

---

*Or: Do you know...?
Could you tell me...?
Could you please tell me...?
Could you possibly tell me...?
Do you have any idea...?
Do you by any chance know...?

Choose

1. I'm not sure ____.
   a. where do you live
   b. where you live

2. They don't know ____.
   a. where the museum is
   b. where is the museum

3. Do you remember ____?
   a. where you put the car keys
   b. where did you put the car keys

4. Could you tell me ____?
   a. why Fred was fired
   b. why was Fred fired

5. I have no idea ____.
   a. how much a concert ticket costs
   b. how much does a concert ticket cost

READING

1. Who was the nineteenth president of the United States?
2. When did the Civil War end?
3. When did California become a state?
4. Where was George Washington born?
5. How many people signed the Declaration of Independence?
6. Where was Abraham Lincoln assassinated?
7. Why was Washington, D.C. chosen as the capital?
8. What did Alexander Graham Bell invent?

A "SURPRISE" QUIZ

Mrs. Murphy is giving her students a "surprise" history quiz today, and Jeffrey isn't very happy about it. He has been absent for the past several days, and he's having a lot of trouble answering the questions.

He doesn't know who the nineteenth president of the United States was. He isn't sure when the Civil War ended. He doesn't remember when California became a state. He has forgotten where George Washington was born. He can't remember how many people signed the Declaration of Independence. He doesn't know where Abraham Lincoln was assassinated. He has forgotten why Washington, D.C. was chosen as the capital. And he has no idea what Alexander Graham Bell invented!

Jeffrey is very upset. He's sure he's going to fail Mrs. Murphy's "surprise" history quiz.

✔CHECK-UP

Q & A

The history quiz is over, and Mrs. Murphy is going over the answers with her students. Using the story as a guide, complete the following conversation.

A. Who knows who the nineteenth president of the United States was?
B. I do. It was Rutherford B. Hayes.
A. And who can tell me _____?
C. I can. It ended in 1865.
A. Does anyone know _____?
D. Yes. It became a state in 1850.
A. Who remembers _____?
E. I remember. He was born in Virginia.
A. Can anybody tell me _____?
F. Yes. It was signed by 56 people.
A. Who knows _____?
G. He was assassinated at Ford's Theater in Washington, D.C.
A. And who can tell me _____?
H. It was chosen because the northern and southern states agreed it was a good location for the capital.
A. And finally, who remembers _____?
I. I do. He invented the telephone.
A. Very good, class!

READING

AT THE MIDTOWN MEDICAL CLINIC

It's a busy afternoon at the Midtown Medical Clinic. Lots of people are sitting in the waiting room and thinking about the questions they're going to ask the doctor.

Frank wants to know if he broke his arm. Mrs. Wilkins needs to know if she has lost too much weight. Arnold wants to find out whether he should go on a diet. Mrs. Parker is wondering whether her children have the measles. Dan is hoping to find out if he'll be able to play in the soccer match next week. Linda is going to ask the doctor whether she has to have her tonsils taken out. Edward expects to find out whether he needs glasses. And Vicki is anxious to know if she's pregnant.

Everybody is waiting patiently, but they hope they don't have to wait too long. They're all anxious to hear the answers to their questions.

✔CHECK-UP

Q & A

The people in the story are registering with the receptionist at the Midtown Medical Clinic. Using this model, create dialogs based on the story.

A. I'd like to see the doctor, please.
B. What seems to be the problem?
A. I'm wondering (if/whether) *I broke my arm.*
B. All right. Please take a seat in the waiting room. The doctor will see you shortly.

Listening

Listen and choose where the conversation is taking place.

1. a. a clinic   b. a hospital
2. a. an office   b. a fire department
3. a. a doctor's office b. a school
4. a. an airport   b. an airplane
5. a. a book store   b. a library

Choose

1. Do you know _____?
   a. is it going to rain
   b. if it's going to rain

2. I'm not really sure _____.
   a. whether the plane will be late
   b. will the plane be late

3. The librarian can tell you _____.
   a. if the library will be open
   b. whether will the library be open

4. Can you tell me _____?
   a. where have they moved
   b. whether they have moved

5. I'm anxious to know _____.
   a. how did I do on the exam
   b. how I did on the exam

6. Jackie is wondering _____.
   a. whether she got the job
   b. did she get the job

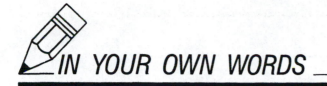

IN YOUR OWN WORDS

For Writing and Discussion

> Do you know...?
> Can you tell me...?
> Could you tell me...?
> Could you please tell me...?
> Could you possibly tell me...?
> Do you have any idea...?
> Do you by any chance know...?
> I'd like to know...
> I'm wondering...

1.

Mr. and Mrs. Grant are planning to move out of their apartment and buy a house. They're visiting a house right now and talking with a real estate agent. What questions should they ask?

They should ask how old the house is.
They should ask whether the roof leaks.
They should ask _____.

Now create a conversation between Mr. and Mrs. Grant and the real estate agent. Use some of the expressions at the top of the page in your questions.

2.

Tina is planning to buy a used car. She's visiting a used car lot right now and talking with a salesman. What questions should she ask?

She should ask whether the brakes work.
She should ask who the previous owner was.
She should ask _____.

Now create a conversation between Tina and the car salesman. Use some of the expressions at the top of the page in your questions.

3.

Michael is planning to go to college next year. He's going to apply to many different schools. He's visiting a college right now and talking with a person in the admissions office. What questions should he ask?

He should ask what courses students have to take.
He should ask if the college has a good library.
He should ask _____.

Now create a conversation between Michael and the person in the admissions office. Use some of the expressions at the top of the page in your questions.

14

Perfect Modals:
Should Have
Must Have
Might Have
May Have
Could Have

They Didn't Do As Well As They Should Have

Lucky People

George Didn't Come to English Class

THEY DIDN'T DO AS WELL AS THEY SHOULD HAVE

Gloria didn't do as well as she should have at a job interview today. She didn't get the job, and she realizes now that she should have done a few things differently. She should have spoken more confidently, she should have told more about her previous experience, and she probably should have worn more conservative clothes.

In addition, she shouldn't have arrived late for the interview. She shouldn't have smoked in the interviewer's office. And she DEFINITELY shouldn't have asked so many questions about vacations and sick days. Gloria will certainly do things differently the next time she has a job interview!

Arthur didn't do as well as he should have at a tennis tournament yesterday. He didn't win, and he realizes now that he should have done a few things differently. He should have practiced more during the week, he should have done more warm-up exercises before the tournament, and he probably should have gotten a good night's sleep the night before.

Furthermore, he shouldn't have used his old tennis racket. He shouldn't have eaten such a large breakfast that morning. And he DEFINITELY shouldn't have gone out dancing with his friends the night before. Arthur will certainly do a few things differently the next time he plays in a tennis tournament!

✓ CHECK-UP

True, False, or Maybe?

Answer True, False, or Maybe (if the answer isn't in the story).

1. Gloria didn't speak confidently about herself at the interview.
2. She didn't get the job because she didn't have previous experience.
3. Gloria likes to go on vacations and gets sick very often.
4. Arthur didn't practice for the tennis tournament.
5. He used his old tennis racket during the tournament.
6. Arthur's friends think that going dancing is more fun than playing tennis.

What's Your Opinion?

1. What should Gloria do the next time she has a job interview?
2. What should Arthur do the next time he plays in a tennis tournament?

Tell about a time when you didn't do as well as you should have. What was the situation? What should you have done differently?

Listening

Listen and choose the best answer based on the conversation you hear.

1. a. He should have spoken softer.
   b. He should have spoken louder.

2. a. They should have gotten there earlier.
   b. They should have left later.

3. a. He should have dressed more comfortably.
   b. He should have spoken more confidently.

4. a. He should have left them in the oven longer.
   b. He should have taken them out of the oven sooner.

5. a. She should have gotten a good night's sleep last night.
   b. She should have gotten up earlier this morning.

6. a. He should have written more legibly.
   b. He should have studied harder.

✏ IN YOUR OWN WORDS

For Writing and Discussion

What should you do if you want to do well at a job interview?

What should you talk about?
What should you ask about?
What should you wear?
What should you bring with you?
When should you arrive?

(In your answers, use "You should.")*

*"You should" = "a person should."

LUCKY PEOPLE

Gary must have been daydreaming while he was driving to work yesterday. He drove through a red light at the busiest intersection in town. Fortunately, he didn't hit anybody. Gary was pretty lucky. He could have caused a terrible accident.

Mrs. Chen must have been very scared yesterday. There was a big, mean dog outside while she was putting out the garbage. Fortunately, the dog was chained to a fence. Mrs. Chen was pretty lucky. She might have been bitten.

Howard must have been extremely irritable yesterday. He got into a big argument with his supervisor over something very unimportant. Fortunately, his supervisor didn't get angry. Howard was very lucky. He could have gotten fired.

Mrs. Wilson must have been feeling very brave this morning. She refused to hand over her purse to a man who was trying to mug her. Fortunately, he got scared and ran away. Mrs. Wilson was very lucky. She might have gotten hurt . . . or even killed!

Mr. and Mrs. Carson must have been having a lot of financial problems last year. They were never able to pay their rent on time. Fortunately, their landlord was very understanding. Mr. and Mrs. Carson were pretty lucky. They could have been evicted.

Irwin must have been very lonely last night. He spent the entire evening making long distance phone calls to his friends all over the country. Fortunately, most of his friends weren't home. Irwin was pretty lucky. He could have run up quite a big phone bill this month.

1. Tell about a time when something bad *could have* happened to you, but *didn't*. What was the situation? What could have happened?

2. Tell about a time when you were . . . . lonely.
. . . . scared.
. . . . irritable.
. . . . brave.

READING

GEORGE DIDN'T COME TO ENGLISH CLASS

George didn't come to his English class yesterday evening, and all the students in the class are wondering why.

Natasha thinks he might have gotten sick. Henry thinks he might have had a doctor's appointment. Mr. and Mrs. Ramirez think that one of George's children may have been sick. Nicole thinks he may have had to work overtime. Mr. and Mrs. Sato think he might have gone to the airport to meet his relatives who are arriving from overseas. And Maria thinks he may have decided to study in another school.

All the students are curious about why George didn't come to English class yesterday evening . . . and they're a little concerned.

IN YOUR OWN WORDS

For Writing and Discussion

Tell a story using this model as a guide.

Our English teacher didn't come to class today, and all the students are wondering why.

_____ thinks _____.
_____ thinks _____.
•
•
•
And I think _____.

We're all curious about why our English teacher didn't come to class today . . . and we're a little concerned.

Conditional:
Present Real
(If ___ Will)
Present Unreal
(If ___ Would)
Hope-Clauses

The Wishing Well

They Would Be Willing to If . . .

THE WISHING WELL

There's a park in the center of Danville, and in the park there's a wishing well. This wishing well is a very popular spot with the people of Danville. Every day people pass by the wishing well, drop in a coin, and make a wish. Some people make wishes about their jobs, others make wishes about the weather, and lots of people make wishes about their families and friends.

Today is a particularly busy day at the wishing well. Many people are coming by and making wishes about their hopes for the future.

Ralph hopes he sells a lot of used cars this month. If he sells a lot of used cars, he'll receive a large Christmas bonus.

Patricia hopes she gets a raise soon. If she gets a raise, her family will be able to take a vacation.

Nancy and Paul hope they find a cheap apartment soon. If they find a cheap apartment, they won't have to live with Paul's parents anymore.

Andy hopes it snows tomorrow. If it snows tomorrow, his school might be closed.

Lana hopes her next movie is a big success. If it's a big success, she'll be rich and famous.

John hopes he gets good grades on his next report card. If he gets good grades, his parents will buy him the radio he has wanted for a long time.

Mr. and Mrs. Clark hope they live to be a hundred. If they live to be a hundred, they'll be able to watch their grandchildren and great-grandchildren grow up.

J.P. Morgan hopes the nation's economy improves next year. If the economy improves next year, his company's profits will increase.

And Wendy hopes she gets accepted into medical school. If she gets accepted into medical school, she'll become a doctor, just like her father and grandfather.

You can see why the wishing well is a very popular spot with the people of Danville. Day after day, people pass by, drop in their coins, and hope that their wishes come true.

✓ CHECK-UP

Q & A

You're talking with the people in the story above. Using this model, create dialogs based on the story.

A. I hope *I sell a lot of used cars this month.*
B. Oh?
A. Yes. If *I sell a lot of used cars, I'll receive a large Christmas bonus.*
B. Oh, really? Well, good luck! I hope *you sell a lot of used cars!*
A. Thanks.

Choose

1. We hope our landlord doesn't _____ our rent.
   a. improve
   b. increase

2. Have you _____ today's mail yet?
   a. received
   b. accepted

3. Jennifer is very smart. She gets good _____ in all her subjects.
   a. grades
   b. cards

4. The company couldn't increase my salary this year, but they gave me a very nice _____.
   a. raise
   b. bonus

5. Arthur hopes his new Broadway play is a big _____.
   a. profit
   b. success

6. The President is very proud of the country's _____.
   a. inflation
   b. economy

READING

THEY WOULD BE WILLING TO IF...

For several months, Mrs. Hopkins has been pressuring her husband, Albert, to go to the dentist, but he refuses to go. The reason is that he can't stand the sound of the dentist's drill. Albert says that if the dentist's drill didn't bother him so much, he would be willing to go to the dentist. Mrs. Hopkins hopes her husband changes his mind and goes to the dentist soon.

For several months, Barbara's family has been encouraging her to ask her boss for a raise, but Barbara refuses to do it. The reason is that she's afraid he might get angry and say "No." Barbara says that if she weren't afraid of her boss's reaction, she would be willing to ask for a raise. Barbara's family hopes she changes her mind and asks for a raise soon.

For several months, Senator Johnson's assistants have been urging him to run for the presidency, but he refuses to do it. The reason is that he doesn't have enough money to pay for all the television commercials and other campaign expenses. Senator Johnson says that if he had sufficient funds, he would be willing to run. Senator Johnson's assistants hope he changes his mind and runs for the presidency soon.

CHECK-UP

Listening

Listen and choose the statement that is true based on what you hear.

1. a. Albert wasn't afraid of the dentist's drill.
    b. Albert is afraid of the dentist's drill.

2. a. Senator Johnson has enough money.
    b. Senator Johnson isn't interested in running for the presidency.

3. a. Mrs. Jones isn't her math teacher.
    b. Mrs. Jones is her math teacher.

4. a. They might receive bonuses.
    b. The company's profits didn't increase.

5. a. He isn't allergic to trees.
    b. He isn't going hiking this weekend.

6. a. He isn't going to the movies tonight.
    b. He doesn't have to work tonight.

Present Unreal Conditional (continued)
Wish-Clauses

Sick and Tired

They Wish They Lived in the City

All Thumbs

READING

SICK AND TIRED

Frank is "sick and tired" of selling insurance! He has been doing that for twenty-eight years. Frank wishes he sold something else. In fact, at this point in his life, he would be willing to sell ANYTHING, as long as it wasn't insurance!

Mrs. Watson is "sick and tired" of teaching seventh-grade math! She has been teaching that subject for the past eighteen years. Mrs. Watson wishes she taught something else. In fact, at this point in her life, she would be willing to teach ANYTHING, as long as it wasn't seventh-grade math!

Jerry is "sick and tired" of writing want ads and obituaries for the *Midville Times*! He has been doing that since 1959. Jerry wishes he wrote something else. In fact, at this point in his life, he'd be willing to write ANYTHING, as long as it wasn't want ads and obituaries!

Susie and her brother are "sick and tired" of eating peanut butter and jelly sandwiches for lunch every day. They have been eating that for lunch every day for the past four years. Susie and her brother wish their mother would give them something else for lunch. In fact, at this point in their lives, they would be willing to eat ANYTHING for lunch, as long as it wasn't peanut butter and jelly sandwiches!

 CHECK-UP

Choose

1. Bob found his job through the ____.
   a. want ads
   b. obituaries

2. I was very ____ when my supervisor shouted at me in front of all the other employees.
   a. jealous
   b. embarrassed

3. Henry ____ the meeting because he had to go to the dentist.
   a. dropped out of
   b. skipped

4. After our house was robbed, I realized how important it is to have ____.
   a. insurance
   b. taxes

5. If you don't visit Aunt Nellie in the hospital, she'll be very ____.
   a. sick and tired
   b. disappointed

6. This is a ____ of me that was painted when I was three years old.
   a. photography
   b. portrait

READING

Mr. Anderson Mrs. Anderson

Michael Jennifer Steven

THEY WISH THEY LIVED IN THE CITY

The Anderson family lives in the suburbs, but they wish they lived in the city. If they lived in the city, Mr. Anderson wouldn't have to spend all his spare time mowing the lawn and working around the house. Mrs. Anderson wouldn't have to spend two hours commuting to work every day. Their son Michael would be able to take the bus to the baseball stadium. Their daughter, Jennifer, would be living close to all of her favorite book stores. And their other son, Steven, could visit the zoo more often. It would be very difficult for the Anderson family to move to the city now, but perhaps some day they'll be able to. They certainly hope so.

✓ CHECK-UP

Listening

Listen and write the missing words.

Mrs. Burton Mr. Burton

Ken Betsy and Kathy Tiger

THEY WISH THEY LIVED IN THE SUBURBS

The Burton family lives in the city, but they _____₁ they lived in the suburbs. If they _____₂ in the suburbs, Mrs. Burton _____₃ be able to plant a garden and grow vegetables. Mr. Burton _____₄ have to listen to the noisy city traffic all the time. Their son, Ken, _____₅ a backyard to play in. Their daughters, Betsy and Kathy, _____₆ share a room. And their cat, Tiger, _____₇ go outside and roam around and play with the other cats. It _____₈ very difficult for the Burton family to move to the suburbs now, but perhaps some day _____₉. They certainly hope so.

How about YOU?

1. Do you wish you lived someplace else? Where? Why?
2. Compare life in the city and life in the suburbs. What are the advantages and disadvantages of each?

ALL THUMBS

Ethel can never fix anything around the house. In fact, everybody tells her she's "all thumbs." She wishes she were more mechanically inclined. If she were more mechanically inclined, she would be able to repair things around the house by herself.

Robert can't dance very well. In fact, all the girls he goes out with tell him he has "two left feet." Robert wishes he could dance better. If he could dance better, he wouldn't feel so self-conscious when he goes out dancing.

Maria is having a hard time learning English. She's having a lot of trouble with English grammar and pronunciation. Maria wishes she had a "better ear" for languages. If she had a "better ear" for languages, she probably wouldn't be having so much trouble in her English class.

✔CHECK-UP

Match

Try to match the following expressions with the descriptions on the right.

_____ 1. He's *handy* around the house.
_____ 2. She has a green *thumb*.
_____ 3. He's very *nosey*.
_____ 4. She shoots from the *hip*.
_____ 5. He's all *heart*.
_____ 6. They've got a lot on their *shoulders*.
_____ 7. He's up in *arms*.
_____ 8. She always keeps her *chin* up.

a. very angry
b. very honest and blunt
c. optimistic
d. knows how to fix things
e. has many responsibilities
f. good at gardening
g. very kind
h. asks about other people

How about YOU?

Are you "all thumbs"? Do you have "two left feet"? Everybody has a few things he or she would like to do better. What do you wish you could do better? Why?

Past Unreal Conditional (If ____ Would Have)
Wish-Clauses (continued)

Unexpected Guests

Wishing It Had Happened Differently

Rumors

READING

UNEXPECTED GUESTS

Melba had a very difficult situation at her house a few days ago. Her relatives from Minneapolis arrived unexpectedly, without any advance notice whatsoever, and they wanted to stay for the weekend.

Needless to say, Melba was very upset. If she had known that her relatives from Minneapolis were going to arrive and want to stay for the weekend, she would have been prepared for their visit. She would have bought a lot of food. She would have cleaned the house. And she certainly wouldn't have invited all her daughter's friends from nursery school to come over and play.

Poor Melba! She really wishes her relatives had called in advance to say they were coming.

✔ CHECK-UP

True, False, or Maybe?

Answer True, False, or Maybe (if the answer isn't in the story).

1. Melba lives in Minneapolis.
2. Her relatives didn't call to say they were coming.
3. If Melba had been prepared for their visit, she probably wouldn't have been upset.
4. When her relatives arrived, Melba was very upset, but she didn't say so.
5. If her house had been clean and she had had more food, Melba would have been more prepared for her relatives' unexpected visit.
6. Melba's relatives realized they should have called in advance to say they were coming.

What's the Word?

Complete these sentences using *would have* or *wouldn't have* and the correct form of the verb.

1. If the plane had arrived on time, I (be) _____ late.
2. If the weather had been nice yesterday, we (go) _____ on a picnic.
3. If I hadn't been out of town, I (miss) _____ the meeting.
4. If I had seen that "stop" sign, Officer, I certainly (drive) _____ through it.
5. If the President hadn't been in a hurry, he (give) _____ a longer speech.

How about YOU?

Have you ever had a difficult situation when something unexpected happened and you weren't prepared? Tell about it.

WISHING IT HAD HAPPENED DIFFERENTLY

Rick forgot to take his notebook home yesterday. He really wishes he had remembered it. If he had remembered it, he would have been able to study last night for today's science test. And if he had been able to study for today's science test, he probably wouldn't have done so badly on it.

Alice's alarm clock didn't ring this morning. She really wishes it had rung. If it had rung, she wouldn't have been late for work this morning. And if she hadn't been late, her supervisor wouldn't have scolded her.

Peter filled out his income tax form very quickly this year. He really wishes he had filled it out more carefully. If he had filled it out more carefully, he wouldn't have made so many mistakes. And if he hadn't made so many mistakes, he wouldn't have gotten into trouble with the Internal Revenue Service.

Mr. and Mrs. Miller didn't follow the directions on the box when they baked brownies yesterday. They really wish they had. If they had followed the directions, they would have used the right ingredients. And if they had used the right ingredients, the brownies probably wouldn't have been as hard as rocks!

✔CHECK-UP

True, False, or Maybe?

Answer True, False, or Maybe (if the answer isn't in the story).

1. Rick didn't do very well on the science test.
2. He wishes he hadn't forgotten his notebook.
3. Alice's supervisor didn't scold her.
4. If Peter hadn't completed the form quickly, he wouldn't have made any mistakes.
5. Mr. and Mrs. Miller's cookies would have been softer if they hadn't used the wrong ingredients.

How about YOU?

Have you ever done something and then regretted it? Tell about something you wish you had done differently, and why.

RUMORS

All the people at the office are talking about Samantha these days. There's a rumor that Samantha is going to get married soon, and everybody is convinced that the rumor is true. After all, if she weren't going to get married soon, she wouldn't be asking everybody about houses for sale in the area. She wouldn't have requested two weeks off next month. And she DEFINITELY wouldn't be wearing a beautiful new ring from her boyfriend!

Of course, the people at the office don't know for sure whether Samantha is going to get married soon. It's only a rumor. They'll just have to wait and see.

All the assembly-line workers at the National Motors automobile factory are worrying about the future these days. There's a rumor that the factory is going to close down soon, and everybody is convinced that the rumor is true. After all, if the factory weren't going to close down soon, everybody on the night shift wouldn't have been laid off. The managers wouldn't all be reading the want ads and working on their resumes. And the boss DEFINITELY wouldn't have canceled the annual company picnic!

Of course, the assembly-line workers at National Motors don't know for sure whether the factory is going to close down soon. It's only a rumor. They'll just have to wait and see.

CHECK-UP

True, False, or Maybe?

Answer True, False, or Maybe (if the answer isn't in the story).

1. Samantha is going to get married soon.
2. Samantha isn't asking about houses in the area.
3. The people at the office think Samantha wouldn't have gotten a new ring if she weren't going to get married.
4. There's a rumor that workers on the night shift at the National Motors factory are going to lose their jobs.
5. There isn't going to be a company picnic this year.
6. If the rumor is true, the factory will close down soon.

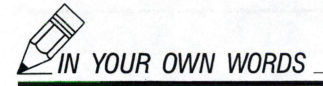

IN YOUR OWN WORDS

For Writing and Discussion

Have you heard any rumors lately at school or at work? Tell a story about a rumor.

What's the rumor?
Do people think the rumor is true?
Why or why not?

CHECK-UP

Choose

1. The students in our class were upset when our teacher quit last week.
   a. We won't be upset if she doesn't quit.
   b. We wouldn't be upset if she didn't quit.
   c. We wouldn't have been upset if she hadn't quit.

2. I didn't come over to your table and have lunch with you because I didn't see you in the cafeteria.
   a. If I saw you, I would have come over and had lunch with you.
   b. If I had seen you, I would have come over and had lunch with you.
   c. If I had seen you, I would come over and have lunch with you.

3. I'm afraid I can't help you type those letters because I'm going to leave work early today.
   a. If I weren't going to leave early today, I'd help you type those letters.
   b. If I were going to leave early today, I'd help you type those letters.
   c. If I were going to leave early today, I wouldn't help you type those letters.

4. Betsy didn't bring her umbrella to work today. She got wet on the way home.
   a. If Betsy hadn't brought her umbrella to work today, she wouldn't have gotten wet.
   b. If Betsy had brought her umbrella to work today, she wouldn't have gotten wet.
   c. If Betsy hadn't brought her umbrella to work today, she would have gotten wet.

Listening

Listen and choose the statement that is true based on what you hear.

1. a. He's rich.
   b. He isn't rich.

2. a. She wrote down his phone number.
   b. She didn't write down his phone number.

3. a. He would have enjoyed the play more if he had sat in a better seat.
   b. He wouldn't have enjoyed the play more if he had sat in a better seat.

4. a. The boys in the hallway aren't the landlord's children.
   b. The boys in the hallway are the landlord's children.

5. a. He didn't get the job he applied for.
   b. He got the job he applied for.

6. a. Johnny's grandparents are at his party.
   b. Johnny's grandparents couldn't come to his party.

18

Reported Speech
Sequence of Tenses

While You Were Gone

The Job Interview

Good Advice

READING

WHILE YOU WERE GONE

Dear Mom,

I'm at my friend Julie's house right now. I'll be home at five. There were a lot of phone calls this afternoon while you were gone.

The plumber called. He said he couldn't fix the bathtub because he was sick.

Grandma called. She said Grandpa was feeling much better today.

Mr. and Mrs. Davis called. They said they wouldn't be able to come to dinner this Saturday night.

The landlord called. He said he hadn't received this month's rent yet.

Cousin Sue called. She said she was sorry she hadn't had time to come over and visit last Saturday.

Uncle Harry called. He said he would call back later.

The neighbors across the street called. They said they had been robbed last night.

And finally, Joe's Auto Repair Shop called. They said they had fixed the radiator but they had found a few things wrong with the engine and it would cost an additional $200.

Love,
Sally

✓ CHECK-UP

Q & A

Sally's mother is working late at the office today. She's calling Sally to find out how things are at home. Create dialogs based on the following model and the information below.

A. Tell me, have there been any calls?
B. Yes. *The plumber* called.
A. Oh? What did *he* say?
B. *He said he was still sick and he couldn't come over today.*

1. Grandma: "Grandpa isn't feeling very well today and wants to call the doctor."
2. Mr. and Mrs. Davis: "Our plans have changed and we CAN come to dinner after all."
3. The landlord: "I received your check this morning."
4. Cousin Sue: "I'll be able to visit you next weekend."
5. Uncle Harry: "I'm getting married and I want all of you to come to my wedding."
6. The neighbors across the street: "The police caught the man who robbed our house."
7. Joe's Auto Repair Shop: "We've finished working on the engine, and the car is ready to be picked up."

■ 88

What's the Word?

Fill in the correct words to complete the story, using the illustration as a guide.

HOME FROM THE NAVY

Bill serves as a lieutenant in the navy. He returned home last weekend after being away at sea for several months. Since he hadn't been in touch with his family for a long time, he was very surprised at all the things that had happened while he was away.

He didn't know his older brother *had gotten* engaged. He also didn't know his sister and brother-in-law _____ _____ _____[1] have a baby. He hadn't heard that his younger brother _____ _____[3] slightly hurt in a car accident. He was unaware that his father _____ _____ _____[4] retire next month.

In addition, he didn't know there _____ _____[5] a big fire at the high school. He hadn't heard that the shoe factory _____ _____[6] and two thousand people _____ _____[7] their jobs. He also hadn't heard that the dog _____ _____[8] six puppies. And he had no idea that his high school sweetheart _____ _____[9] a movie star and _____ _____[10] to Hollywood.

A lot of things certainly had changed while Bill was away.

True, False, or Maybe?

Answer True, False, or Maybe (if the answer isn't in the story).

1. Bill has been on a ship for the past several months.
2. His sister had a baby while he was away.
3. His younger brother wasn't hurt very badly when he was in a car accident recently.
4. Bill's high school was very large.
5. Bill's former girlfriend lives in Hollywood now.

Listening

Listen and choose the statement that is true based on what you hear.

1. a. He didn't know that his supervisor had been in the hospital.
   b. He didn't know that his supervisor was in the hospital.

2. a. It's snowing.
   b. It snowed.

3. a. He wasn't aware that jackets were on sale.
   b. He didn't know jackets had been on sale.

4. a. She didn't know he had to work on Saturday.
   b. She didn't know he had worked on Saturday.

5. a. She was aware that Roger had been thinking of leaving.
   b. She was unaware that Roger had been thinking of leaving.

6. a. Her friends hadn't told her they were going to move.
   b. Her friends had told her they were going to move.

Speech bubbles (illustration):

Where did you go to school?

Have you had any special training?

Where have you worked?

Are you willing to move to another city?

Can you work overtime and weekends?

How is your health?

Have you ever been fired?

Why did you have four different jobs in the past year?

Why do you think you're more qualified for the position than the other sixty-two people who have applied?

UNITED INSURANCE COMPANY

THE JOB INTERVIEW

Charles had a job interview a few days ago at the United Insurance Company. The interview lasted almost an hour, and Charles had to answer a lot of questions.

First, the interviewer asked Charles where he had gone to school. Then, she asked if he had had any special training. She asked where he had worked. She also asked whether he was willing to move to another city. She wanted to know if he could work overtime and weekends. She asked him how his health was. She asked him whether he had ever been fired. She wanted to know why he had had four different jobs in the past year.

And finally, the interviewer asked the most difficult question. She wanted to know why Charles thought he was more qualified for the position than the other sixty-two people who had applied.

Charles had never been asked so many questions at a job interview before. He doesn't know how well he did, but he tried his best.

✓ CHECK-UP

Q & A

You're applying for a job at the United Insurance Company. Role-play a job interview with another student, using the questions in the illustration as a guide.

How about YOU?

1. Tell about a job interview you have had.
   Where was the interview?
   How long did it last?
   What questions did the interviewer ask?
   What were your answers?
   What was the most difficult question, and how did you answer it?
   Did you get the job?

2. Job interviewers sometimes like to ask difficult questions. Why do you think they do this? What are some difficult questions interviewers might ask? Make a list and think of answers to these questions.

GOOD ADVICE

Margaret had a bad stomachache yesterday afternoon. She called her doctor and asked him what she should do. Her doctor told her to rest in bed. He also told her not to eat too much for dinner. And he told her to call him in the morning if she was still sick. Margaret felt better after speaking with her doctor. She's glad she can always depend on him for good advice.

Eric went out on his first date yesterday evening. Before he left the house, he asked his parents if they had any advice. They told him to be polite when he met the girl's mother and father. They also told him not to drive too fast. And they told him not to bring his date home any later than ten o'clock. Eric felt more prepared for his date after speaking with his parents. He's glad he can always depend on them for good advice.

The day before Mrs. Benson's students took their college entrance examination, they asked Mrs. Benson if she had any helpful advice. She told them to answer the questions quickly but carefully. She also told them not to get nervous. And she told them to get a good night's sleep before the test. Mrs. Benson's students felt more confident after speaking with her. They're glad they can always depend on her for good advice.

Mr. and Mrs. Newton are going away on vacation soon and are a little concerned because there have been several robberies in their neighborhood recently. They called the police and asked them what they could do to prevent their house from being broken into while they were away. The police told them to lock all the windows and leave on a few lights. They also advised them to ask the neighbors to pick up the mail. And they warned them not to tell too many people that they would be away. Mr. and Mrs. Newton felt reassured after speaking with the police. They're glad they can always depend on them for good advice.

IN YOUR OWN WORDS

For Writing and Discussion

Tell about some situations in which people have given you good advice. For each situation, answer these questions:

Why did you need advice?
Who did you ask, and what did you ask?
What did the person tell you?

19

Tag Questions
Emphatic Sentences

A Broken Engagement

Unfair Accusations

A BROKEN ENGAGEMENT

Dear John,

It's been a long time since I have written to you, hasn't it. I'm sorry it has taken me such a long time to write, but I really don't know where to begin this letter. You see, John, things have been very difficult since you took that job overseas several months ago. It has been very difficult for me to be engaged to somebody who is four thousand miles away, so I have decided that things have got to change.

I have decided to move out of my parents' house. I'm going to get my own apartment.

I have already started dating other guys.

I want to break our engagement.

And I gave your mother back the ring you had given me.

I'm sorry things have to end this way. You DO understand why I must do this, don't you?

Sincerely,   Jane

Dear Jane,

I received your letter today and I couldn't believe what you had written.

You haven't really decided to move out of your parents' house, have you?

You aren't really going to get your own apartment, are you?

You haven't really started dating other guys, have you?

You don't really want to break our engagement, do you?

And you didn't really give my mother back the ring I had given you, did you?

Please answer me as soon as possible!

Love,
John

P.S. You DO still love me, don't you?

Dear John,

I HAVE decided to move out of my parents' house.

I AM going to get my own apartment.

I HAVE already started dating other guys.

I DO want to break our engagement.

And I DID give your mother back the ring you had given me.

I know this must hurt, but I DO have to be honest with you, don't I. I hope that someday you will understand.

Good-bye,
Jane

✓ CHECK-UP

Answer These Questions

1. Why did Jane decide to break her engagement to John?
2. Where has Jane been living?
3. What had Jane done with the ring that John had given her?
4. How did John feel when he received Jane's first letter?
5. Did Jane realize how John would feel when he received her second letter?

Choose

1. John wanted to know if Jane ____ to break their engagement.
   a. had really decided
   b. has really decided

2. John asked Jane whether she ____ her own apartment.
   a. had really gotten
   b. was really going to get

3. In her first letter, Jane said she ____ break their engagement.
   a. wants to
   b. wanted to

4. John was hoping she ____ him.
   a. still loved
   b. had still loved

5. In Jane's second letter, she told John she really ____ to move out of her parents' house.
   a. has decided
   b. had decided

6. She told him she hoped that someday he ____.
   a. would have understood
   b. would understand

✏ IN YOUR OWN WORDS

For Writing and Discussion

John is willing to do anything he can to save his relationship with Jane. He has some ideas about how to do this, and he's going to write to her one more time. Write John's letter to Jane.

UNFAIR ACCUSATIONS

> **To:** Michael Parker
> **From:** Ms. Lewis
> **Re:** Your Performance at Work
>
> I'm concerned about your performance at work.
>
> You have been working too slowly.
>
> You often get to work late.
>
> You took too many sick days last month.
>
> You aren't very polite to the customers.
>
> And you don't get along well with the other employees.
>
> I'd like to meet with you as soon as possible to discuss this.

Michael's boss, Ms. Lewis, sent him a memo recently about his performance at work. In the memo, she said he had been working too slowly. She also said that he often got to work late. In addition, she observed that he had taken too many sick days the month before. She also mentioned that he wasn't very polite to the customers. And finally, she complained that he didn't get along well with the other employees.

When Michael got the memo, he was very upset. He feels that his boss is making unfair accusations. Michael feels that he HASN'T been working too slowly. He also feels that he DOESN'T often get to work late. In Michael's opinion, he DIDN'T take too many sick days last month. He thinks he IS polite to the customers. And he maintains that he DOES get along well with the other employees.

Michael realizes that he and his boss see things VERY differently, and he plans to speak to her about this as soon as possible.

☑ CHECK-UP

Match

Match the descriptions of job performance on the left with their meanings.

____ 1. efficient	a. pleasant and outgoing
____ 2. honest	b. easy to work with
____ 3. punctual	c. works quickly and accurately
____ 4. industrious	d. thoughtful of others
____ 5. cooperative	e. tells the truth
____ 6. friendly	f. does things on time
____ 7. considerate	g. cares about the work
____ 8. dedicated	h. works hard

Listening

Listen and decide who is speaking.

1. a. tenant–tenant
   b. tenant–mailman

2. a. student–student
   b. student–teacher

3. a. salesperson–customer
   b. wife–husband

4. a. employee–employee
   b. student–student

5. a. passenger–driver
   b. police officer–driver

6. a. doctor–nurse
   b. doctor–patient

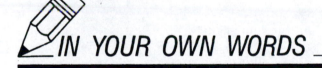 IN YOUR OWN WORDS

For Writing and Discussion

```
                 MEMO

To:
From:
Re:
```

Mr. Hopper is very pleased with Helen Baxter's performance at work. Using the story below as a guide, write a memo from Mr. Hopper to Helen Baxter.

POSITIVE FEEDBACK

Helen Baxter's boss, Mr. Hopper, sent her a memo recently about her job performance. He said that he was very pleased with her performance at work. He mentioned that she was very efficient and industrious. He observed that she got along well with her co-workers and customers. And he also said that she was very cooperative and considerate. Mr. Hopper wrote that the company had been so pleased with her work that they were going to give her a big raise.

20

Review:
Verb Tenses
Conditionals
A Bad Day

A BAD DAY

Marcia made several bad decisions yesterday.

She decided to drive to work, but she should have taken the train. If she had taken the train, she wouldn't have gotten stuck in a terrible traffic jam.

She decided to have lunch with a friend at a small restaurant far from her office, but she should have gone to a place nearby. If she had gone to a place nearby, she wouldn't have been an hour late for an important afternoon appointment.

She decided not to take the garbage out until after she got home from work that evening, but she should have taken it out in the morning. If she had taken it out in the morning, her cat wouldn't have tipped over the garbage pail and made such a mess all over the kitchen.

And finally, that evening she decided to stay up late and watch a scary movie on TV, but she should have turned off the TV and gone to sleep. If she had turned off the TV and gone to sleep, she wouldn't have had terrible nightmares all night.

Marcia certainly didn't have a very good day yesterday. As a matter of fact, she probably shouldn't even have gotten out of bed in the first place. If she hadn't gotten out of bed in the first place, none of this would have ever happened!

✔CHECK-UP

True, False, or Maybe?

Answer True, False, or Maybe (if the answer isn't in the story).

1. Marcia probably wishes she had taken the train to work yesterday.
2. If Marcia hadn't had lunch far from her office, she would have been on time for her appointment.
3. There aren't any small restaurants near Marcia's office.
4. She decided not to take the garbage out in the morning.
5. If there hadn't been a scary movie on TV, Marcia would have gone to sleep.

How about YOU?

We all sometimes make decisions we later wish we hadn't made. Tell about some bad decisions you have made over the years.
> What did you decide to do?
> What should you have done?
> Why?

Listening

Listen and choose where the conversation is taking place.

1. a. department store
   b. laundromat

2. a. restaurant
   b. someone's home

3. a. bus
   b. movie theater

4. a. supermarket
   b. cafeteria

5. a. shopping mall
   b. park

6. a. airplane
   b. concert

Choose

1. If I _____ you were going to be in town, I would have invited you to stay at our house.
   a. knew
   b. had known

2. If _____ busy tonight, I'll call you.
   a. I weren't
   b. I'm not

3. If I _____ the plane, I probably would have gotten there faster.
   a. had taken
   b. took

4. I _____ happy to go skiing with you if you asked me.
   a. would be
   b. would have been

5. If I were you, I _____ that movie.
   a. wouldn't see
   b. would have seen

6. I wish I _____ when I was young.
   a. learned to swim
   b. had learned to swim

7. If I had been more careful, I _____ driven through that stop sign.
   a. would have
   b. wouldn't have

8. I think anybody would get tired of eating in restaurants if they _____ in restaurants all the time.
   a. eat
   b. ate

101

Tape Scripts for Listening Exercises

Chapter 1 – p. 3

Listen and choose the best answer.

1. What are you doing?
2. Do you swim very often?
3. Are you a good cook?
4. What's Tom cooking?
5. Who cooks in your family?
6. Do they like to study?
7. Does he want to be a violinist?
8. Are you and your brother busy this afternoon?
9. Does Mrs. King like to swim?
10. What's Peter reading?

Chapter 2 – p. 8

Listen and choose the best answer.

1. Did you do well at your job interview yesterday?
2. What did your children do this morning?
3. What was she doing when she broke her arm?
4. What was his supervisor doing?
5. Sally, why did you fall asleep during class?
6. Why didn't you finish your dinner?

Chapter 3 – p. 10

Listen to the conversation and choose the answer that is true.

1. A. Don't wear your blue suit tonight. You wore it last weekend.
   B. All right. Where's my BLACK suit?
2. A. Do we need anything from the supermarket?
   B. Yes. We need some beef, some potatoes, and some tomatoes.
3. A. Which movie do you want to see?
   B. How about "The Man in the Brown Suit"?
   A. Okay. What channel is it on?
4. A. What are you going to do tomorrow?
   B. I'm going to plant lettuce, tomatoes, and beans.
5. A. What's the matter with it?
   B. The brakes don't work, and it doesn't start very well in the morning.
6. A. This car is very nice, but it's too expensive.
   B. You're right.

Chapter 4 – p. 16

1. *Sharon is on vacation in San Francisco. She's checking her list of things to do while she's on vacation. On the list below, check the things Sharon has already done.*

   Sharon has already seen the Golden Gate Bridge. She hasn't visited Golden Gate Park yet. She took a tour of Alcatraz Prison yesterday. She's going to go to Chinatown tomorrow. She's eaten at Fisherman's Wharf, and she hasn't had time to buy souvenirs yet.

2. *Alan is a secretary in a very busy office. He's checking his list of things to do before 5 P.M. on Friday. On the list below, check the things Alan has already done.*

   Alan has called Mrs. Porter. He has to type the letter to the Ajax Insurance Company. He's gone to the bank. He hasn't taken the mail to the post office. He cleaned the coffee machine, and he's going to speak to the boss about his salary.

3. *It's Saturday, and Judy and Paul Johnson are doing lots of things around the house. They're checking the list of things they have to do today. On the list below, check the things they've already done.*

   Judy and Paul haven't done the laundry. They have to wash the kitchen windows. They've paid the bills. They'll clean the garage later. They couldn't fix the bathroom sink, but they vacuumed the living room.

Chapter 5 – p. 20

Listen to the conversation and choose the answer that is true.

1. A. How long have you had a toothache?
   B. For three days.
2. A. How long was your knee swollen?
   B. For a week.
3. A. Has your father always been an engineer?
   B. No, he hasn't.
4. A. How long have you known how to skate?
   B. Since I was a teenager.
5. A. Did you live in Rome for a long time?
   B. Yes. Five years.
6. A. How long has Jim been interested in Greek literature?
   B. Since he lived in Greece.
7. A. Is Betty still in the hospital?
   B. Oh, I forgot to tell you. She's been home for two days.
8. A. Have you liked country music for a long time?
   B. Yes. I've liked country music since I moved to Nashville seven years ago.

Chapter 6 – p. 25

I. Listen and decide who is speaking.

1. What a day! All day the tenants have been complaining that nothing is working.
2. I'm very tired. I've given six lessons today.
3. It's been a long day. I've been selling tickets since ten A.M.
4. I'm really tired. I've been watching them all day.
5. Thank you! You've been a wonderful audience!
6. I'm exhausted! I've been looking at paychecks since early this morning.

II. Listen and choose the word you hear.

1. She's gone to sleep.
2. I've never written so many letters in one day before.
3. I've been seeing patients all day.
4. What courses have you taken this year?
5. Is Henry giving blood?
6. Ben has driven all night.

Chapter 7 – p. 32

Listen and choose the best answer.

1. A. I avoid driving downtown whenever I can.
   B. Me, too.
2. A. I've decided to sell my car.
   B. Your beautiful car?
3. A. Please try to quit biting your nails.
   B. Okay, Mom.
4. A. We're thinking about moving to California.
   B. Oh. That's interesting.
5. A. I've been considering getting married for a long time.
   B. Oh, really? I didn't know that.
6. A. Don't stop practicing!
   B. Okay.

Chapter 8 – p. 37

Listen and choose the best answer.

1. I hadn't seen that movie before.
2. I haven't gone swimming in years.
3. Has the play started yet?
4. Michael, please go upstairs and do your homework!
5. Why did Carmen do well on the History test?
6. I enjoyed dinner at Stanley's Restaurant last night.

Chapter 9 – p. 41

Listen and write the missing words.

Dear Alice,

   I'm very discouraged. I'm having a lot of trouble with my girlfriend and I don't know what to do. The problem is very simple: I'm in love with her, but she isn't in love with me! A few weeks ago, I gave her a ring, but she gave it back. During the past few months I have written several love letters to her, but she has thrown them away. Recently I asked her to marry me. She thought it over for a while, and then she turned me down. Now when I try to call her up she doesn't even want to talk to me. Please try to help me. I don't know what to do.

"Discouraged Donald"
Denver, Colorado

Chapter 9 – p. 44

Listen and choose what the people are talking about.

1. A. Have you filled it out yet?
   B. No, I'm having some trouble. Can you help me?
2. A. Where can I try them on?
   B. The dressing room is right over there.
3. A. Now remember, you can't bring them back!
   B. I understand.
4. A. Please drop them off at the school by eight o'clock.
   B. By eight o'clock? Okay.
5. A. Where should I hang them up?
   B. What about over the fireplace?
6. A. Have you thought it over?
   B. Yes, I have.
7. A. It's cold in here.
   B. You're right. I'll turn it on.
8. A. Should we use it up?
   B. No, let's throw it out.

Chapter 10 – p. 47

Listen and choose what the people are talking about.

1. A. To tell the truth, I'm a little shy.
   B. What a coincidence! I am, too.
2. A. I enjoy going to plays and concerts.
   B. We're very compatible. So do I.
3. A. I'm enjoying this course.
   B. I am, too.
4. A. I'm from Minnesota.
   B. That's interesting. So am I.
5. A. I'm opposed to using animals in scientific experiments.
   B. I am, too.

Chapter 11 – p. 54

Listen and choose the best line to continue the conversation.

1. The dishes haven't been done yet.
2. The packages have been sent.
3. Out cat was bitten by our dog.
4. Sally was invited to John's birthday party.
5. Mrs. Brown hired Mr. Simon as a secretary.
6. Mrs. Davis was hired by Ms. Clark as a computer programmer.
7. Hello. This is Betty's Repair Shop. Your TV has been repaired.
8. Hello. This is Joe's Auto Repair Shop. I'm sorry. We've been very busy. I'm calling to tell you your car is finally being repaired.

Chapter 12 – p. 59

Listen and choose what the people are talking about.

1. A. You really should try it. You'll feel much slimmer and more energetic in just a few days.
   B. Really? I think I will try it.
2. A. He's looking healthier and working faster than he ever has before.
   B. You're right. I've noticed that, too.
3. A. New ones are more reliable than used ones.
   B. That's true. They are.
4. A. Here! Take as many as you want!
   B. Thanks. I appreciate it.
5. A. How do you like it?
   B. It's very good, but I think you used too much flour.

Chapter 13 – p. 64

Listen and choose where the conversation is taking place.

1. A. Do you know how much longer I'll have to stay here?
   B. Just a few more days.
   A. Oh, good.
2. A. Can you tell me why I was fired?
   B. Yes. Everybody in your department was laid off.
   A. Oh, I see.
3. A. Who knows how their lungs work?
   B. I do.
   A. Please tell us.
4. A. Do you by any chance know whether we'll be arriving soon?
   B. Yes. We'll be arriving in ten minutes.
   A. Thank you.
5. A. Could you please tell me if this book is on sale?
   B. Yes, it is.

Chapter 14 – p. 69

Listen and choose the best answer based on the conversation you hear.

1. A. I couldn't hear a word he said.
   B. I couldn't, either.
2. A. By the time we got to the party, everyone had left.
   B. That's too bad.
3. A. I just interviewed a young man for the bookkeeper's position.
   B. What did you think of him?
   A. Well, he was very shy and quiet, and he was wearing a T-shirt, jeans, and sneakers.
4. A. I smell smoke!
   B. Oh, no! The cookies are burning!
5. A. I was so tired last night that I slept twelve hours and was late for work this morning.
   B. Oh. I hope the boss wasn't angry.
6. A. Could you tell me how I did on the exam?
   B. Not very well, Richard.

Chapter 15 – p. 76

Listen and choose the statement that is true based on what you hear.

1. If Albert weren't afraid of the dentist's drill, he'd go to the dentist.
2. If Senator Johnson had enough money, he'd be interested in running for the presidency.
3. I'd be very happy if Mrs. Jones were my math teacher.
4. If the company's profits increase, we'll receive bonuses.
5. If I weren't allergic to trees, I'd go hiking.
6. If I didn't have to work tonight, I'd invite you to go to the movies with me.

Chapter 16 – p. 79

Listen and write the missing words.

   The Burton family lives in the city, but they wish they lived in the suburbs. If they lived in the suburbs, Mrs. Burton would be able to plant a garden and grow vegetables. Mr. Burton wouldn't have to listen to the noisy city traffic all the time. Their son, Ken, would have a backyard to play in. Their daughters, Betsy and Kathy, might not have to share a room. And their cat, Tiger, would be able to go outside and roam around and play with the other cats. It would be very difficult for the Burton family to move to the suburbs now, but perhaps some day they'll be able to. They certainly hope so.

Chapter 17 – p. 85

Listen and choose the statement that is true based on what you hear.

1. A. If I were rich, I'd travel around the world.
   B. Really? That sounds like fun!
2. A. Why didn't you call me?
   B. I would have called you if I hadn't forgotten to write down your phone number.
3. A. How did you enjoy the play?
   B. It was all right, but I wish I could have sat in a better seat.
4. A. Those boys are making a lot of noise in the hallway again.
   B. I know. It's terrible. If they weren't the landlord's children, I'd tell them to be quiet.
5. A. You know, I wish I had taken a computer course when I was in college.
   B. Why do you say that?
   A. If I had, I would have gotten the job I applied for.
6. A. Happy Birthday, Johnny! Now blow out the candles and make a wish.
   B. I wish Grandma and Grandpa were here for my birthday party.

Chapter 18 – p. 89

Listen and choose the statement that is true based on what you hear.

1. A. Have you heard the news?
   B. No. What?
   A. Our supervisor is in the hospital.
   B. Oh. I didn't know that. That's too bad.
2. A. I've been in the office all day. I wasn't aware that it had snowed.
   B. I wasn't, either.
3. A. Do you know about our special sale?
   B. No, I don't.
   A. You can buy two jackets for the price of one this week.
   B. No kidding! That's great!
4. A. Hello.
   B. Hello, Barbara? This is Jim. I'm afraid I won't be able to have dinner with you on Saturday. I have to work.
   A. Oh. That's too bad.
5. A. Roger quit his job!
   B. Really? What a surprise!
6. A. We've moved!
   B. Oh. I didn't know that. Where to?
   A. The other side of town.

Chapter 19 – p. 97

Listen and decide who is speaking.

1. A. The mail isn't here yet, is it?
   B. No. Not yet.
   A. That's what I thought.
2. A. I did well on my exam, didn't I?
   B. No, you didn't
   A. I didn't?! I'm really surprised.
3. A. You know . . . That suit looks very good on you.
   B. Come to think of it, you're right! It DOES look very good on me, doesn't it.
   A. Yes, it does. I wonder if it's on sale.
   B. Let's ask somebody.

4. A. You've received our supervisor's memo, haven't you?
   B. Yes, I have.
5. A. You were driving over seventy miles per hour, weren't you?
   B. I guess I was. Are you going to give me a ticket?
6. A. I have some good news!
   B. What is it?
   A. You're fine. You can go home tomorrow.
   B. I CAN?!
   A. Yes. You CAN.
   B. I'm very glad to hear that.

Chapter 20 – p. 101

Listen and choose where the conversation is taking place.

1. A. Excuse me. You just put my shirts in your machine.
   B. I did?
   A. Yes, you did.
2. A. Do you realize what you just did?
   B. No. What did I just do?
   A. You put too much pepper in the soup. Our guests will be sneezing all night.
   B. Oh. I'm sorry. I must have been daydreaming.
3. A. I'm sorry. I must have thought this seat was mine.
   B. That's okay. Don't worry about it. I'm getting off soon anyway.
4. A. What are you going to have?
   B. I'm not sure. If I hadn't had the chicken every day last week, I'd have the chicken.
5. A. You know, I really don't feel like shopping today. Could we go someplace else and take a walk?
   B. Sure. That's fine with me.
6. A. If I had known this was going to be so boring, I wouldn't have bought a ticket.
   B. I agree. I wouldn't have bought one, either.

Index

A
Adverbs, **59**

C
Comparative
    of adjectives, **59**
    of adverbs, **59**
Conditional
    Past unreal (If __ would
      have), **82, 83, 85, 100-101**
    Present real
      (If __ will), **74-75**
    Present unreal
      (If __ could), **80**
      (If __ would), **76, 79, 80, 84-85, 101**
Connectors
    But, **49**
    Either/Neither, **48**
    So/Too, **46-47**
Could have, **70-71**
Count/Non-count nouns, **58**

E
Either, **48**
Embedded questions, **62, 63, 64-65**
Emphatic sentences, **95, 96-97**

F
Fewer, **58**
For, **18-19, 20**

G
Gerunds/Infinitives, **28, 29, 30-32**
Going to + verb, **10**

H
Have to, **25**
Hope-clauses, **74-75**

I
If __ could, **80**
If/Whether, **90**
If __ will, **74-75**
If __ would, **76, 79, 80, 84-85, 101**
If __ would have, **82, 83, 85, 100-101**
Infinitives/Gerunds, **28, 29, 30-32**

M
Many, **58**
Might have, **70-71**
Much, **58**
Must have, **70**

N
Neither, **48**

P
Passive voice
    Past, **52, 53**
    Present continuous, **54**
    Present perfect vs. past, **55**
Perfect modals
    Could have, **70-71**
    Might have, **70-71**
    Must have, **70**
    Should have, **68-69**
Perfect tenses
    Past perfect, **34-35, 36-37**
    Past perfect continuous, **38**
    Present perfect, **14, 15, 16, 18-19, 20, 21**
    Present perfect continuous, **24, 25**
    Present perfect continuous vs. Present perfect, **25**
    Present perfect vs. Past, **21**
    Present perfect vs. Present, **20**
Present continuous tense, **5-6**

R
Reported speech/Sequence of tenses, **88-89, 90, 91, 96-97**

S
Sequence of tenses/Reported speech, **88-89, 90, 91, 96-97**
Should, **69**
Should have, **68-69, 100-101**
Simple past tense, **6**
Simple past vs. Past continuous, **6-8**

Simple present tense, **5-6**
Simple present vs. Present continuous, **5-6**
Since, **18-19, 20**
So, **46-47**
Superlatives, **60**

T
Tag questions, **94-95**
Tenses
    Future: Going to, **10**
    Future: Will, **11**
    Past perfect, **34-35, 36-37**
    Past perfect continuous, **38**
    Present continuous, **5-6**
    Present perfect, **14, 15, 16, 18-19, 20, 21**
    Present perfect continuous, **24, 25**
    Present perfect continuous vs. Present perfect, **25**
    Present perfect vs. Past, **21**
    Present perfect vs. Present, **20**
    Simple past, **6**
    Simple past vs. Past continuous, **6-8**
    Simple present, **5-6**
    Simple present vs. Present continuous, **5-6**
Too, **46-47**
Two-word verbs
    Inseparable, **42, 43-44**
    Separable, **40, 41, 43-44**

W
Whether/If, **90**
Will (present real conditional), **74-75**
Wish-clauses, **78, 79, 80**
Would (present unreal conditional), **76, 78, 79, 80, 84-85, 101**
Would have (past unreal conditional), **82, 83, 85, 100-101**